GET

D1085852

ARABIC

**A quick beginners' course for
tourists and businesspeople**

Course writers: Salah El-Ghobashy
Principal Lecturer in Arabic,
Polytechnic of Central London

Hilary Wise
Lecturer in Linguistics,
Queen Mary College,
University of London

Producer: Alan Wilding

BARRON'S / NEW YORK

By arrangement with the British Broadcasting Corporation

First U.S. Edition published 1986 by Barron's
Educational Series, Inc.

By arrangement with the British Broadcasting
Corporation, 35 Marylebone High Street, London
W1M 4AA.

All inquiries should be addressed to:
Barron's Educational Series, Inc.
250 Wireless Boulevard
Hauppauge, New York 11788

International Standard Book No. 0-8120-2720-5

PRINTED IN THE UNITED STATES OF AMERICA

123   9876543

Contents

		page
Map of the Arab world		4
The course. . . . . . . and how to use it		5
Guide to pronunciation		8
Chapter 1	**Meeting people** Greetings; farewells; how are you?; saying where you're from; what your job is; "see you tomorrow"	13
Chapter 2	**Eating and drinking** Ordering tea, coffee and fruit juice; asking if they sell beer; ordering a complete meal	22
Chapter 3	**Shopping** Asking the price of souvenirs; buying postcards and stamps; bargaining	31
Chapter 4	**In the hotel** Booking a room; saying what facilities you want; using the phone; making an appointment; changing money	42
Chapter 5	**Out and about** Asking the way; finding out train times; using taxis; buying a train ticket	50
Chapter 6	**Business and pleasure** Saying which languages you speak; being invited to someone's home	60
Can you "Get by"?		68
Reference section		71
Answers		76
Word list		82
An introduction to Arabic writing		86

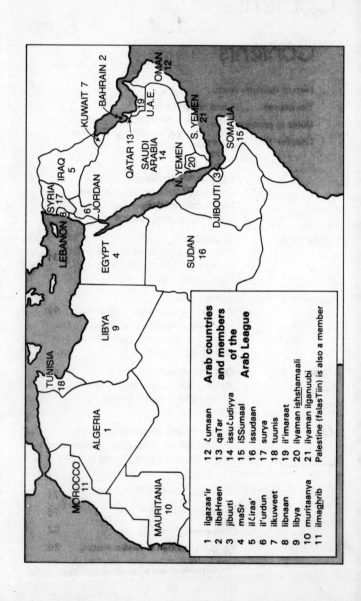

Arab countries and members of the Arab League

1 ilgazaa'ir
2 ilbaHreen
3 jibuuti
4 maSr
5 il؏iraa'
6 il'urdun
7 ilkuweet
8 libnaan
9 libya
10 muritaanya
11 ilmaghrib
12 ؏umaan
13 qaTar
14 issu؏udiyya
15 iSSumaal
16 issudaan
17 surya
18 tuunis
19 il'imaraat
20 ilyaman ishshamaali
21 ilyaman ilganuubi
Palestine (falasTiin) is also a member

The course ...
and how to use it

Get by in Arabic is a six-programme radio course for anyone planning to visit an Arabic-speaking country. It offers a basic 'survival kit' for dealing with the kinds of situation likely to arise on a visit abroad and assumes no previous knowledge of the language.

About Arabic

About 180 million people speak Arabic as their first language. As the language of the Koran, it is also learnt by many millions of Moslems throughout the world.

Arabic is sometimes thought to be a 'difficult' language, perhaps because it is written in an unfamiliar script. So in this book, we have used a writing system based on the Roman alphabet to represent the sounds of the language.

In Arab countries, courtesy and sociability are highly valued, and this is reflected in the language. It abounds in polite expressions, appropriate to particular situations, and any foreigner making the effort to speak Arabic will be welcomed with added warmth and hospitality.

What kind of Arabic?

There are basically two kinds of Arabic: literary and spoken. Literary Arabic is used as the written medium throughout the Arab world, and is spoken on the more formal occasions — in speeches, sermons, news broadcasts and so on. But for all everyday purposes — at home, in shops and offices — colloquial Arabic is used. The area of the Arab world is so vast (three times larger than the whole of Europe from Finland to Spain and from Ireland to Greece) that, not surprisingly, the language varies from country to country.

There are a number of reasons for choosing Egyptian Arabic. Geographically and historically Egypt lies at the heart of the Arab world. Its population (49 million) by far exceeds that of any other Arab country. Practically everyone in the Arab world is exposed, directly or indirectly, to Egyptian Arabic. Films, cassettes of popular songs and television soap operas are exported on a massive scale to other Arab countries. It is generally held to be the most prestigious spoken variety and whichever country you visit you will find people can understand and adapt to Egyptian Arabic.

However, the course also includes some non-Egyptian words which are in widespread use throughout the Arab world. These are given in the additional vocabulary and shown in square brackets.

The programmes

- are based on real-life conversations specially recorded in Cairo, so you get used to hearing everyday Arabic right from the start.
- enable you to cope with confidence in basic day-to-day situations such as meeting people, eating out, shopping and bargaining, travelling around, finding a room, making an appointment, and so on.

The book includes

- an introduction to the sounds of Arabic
- the key words and phrases for each programme
- the texts of the conversations in the order they appear in the programmes
- short explanations of the language
- extra useful vocabulary for each basic situation and background information about life in Arab countries

- exercises to test what you've learnt
- a reference section including language notes, the key to exercises, an introduction to the Arabic script for the really adventurous, and an Arabic-English word-list

The two cassettes

- contain an expanded form of the programmes and extra conversations and exercises. The key words in the 'Guide to pronunciation' section are given at the start of Cassette 1, so you can hear and imitate them while getting to know the writing system we have used; spoken answers to the exercises and test in this book are also given.
- give you the chance to go at your own pace, and take your study of the language a stage further, if you wish.

To make the most of the course

The way you use the course will depend on you and whether you're using the cassettes or the programmes or both. Here are some suggestions:

- If you have the cassettes, practise the key words given at the start of Cassette 1, which are printed on p12.

- *Before each programme,* look at the key words and phrases at the beginning of each chapter, and practise saying them aloud. Read the conversations aloud several times, with someone else if possible. Check the meaning of any words you don't know. Words appearing for the first time are given after the dialogues, otherwise you can check in the full word-list at the end of the book. Then read the explanations provided.

- *During each programme,* listen to the conversations *without looking at the book* and concentrate on the sounds of the language. When you're asked to repeat a word or phrase, try saying it aloud and confidently; this will help you to remember the expressions and to learn to say them with the proper stress. On the cassettes the pauses may seem a little short at first; if so, stop the tape.

- *After each programme,* read through the conversations aloud again. If you have the cassettes, you may find it useful to imitate the conversations phrase by phrase. Check again on the language explanations, then work through the exercises.

- *Making the most of the cassettes:* besides the dialogues and explanations expanding on the programmes, the cassettes contain additional conversations and exercises to reinforce what you've already learnt, and extend your vocabulary. Some of the exercises will draw on the additional vocabulary given at the end of each chapter. So if you make full use of the cassettes you can take your Arabic well beyond the stage of 'getting by'.

Guide to pronunciation

Arabic has its own alphabet of 28 letters, and an introduction to the Arabic script is given on p86. In this book, though, we have used a modified form of the Roman alphabet. The following is a guide to the written symbols we are using and the sounds they represent. The description of sounds relate to standard southern English.

Contrary to general belief, most of the sounds of Arabic are similar to those found in English; only about half a dozen will be unfamiliar to English speakers (and two of these occur relatively infrequently anyway).

- The vowels

  There are three short vowels:

  a   like the vowel in English 'hat' or 'back', as in **gamal** (camel)

  i   like the vowel in 'hit' or 'ship', as in **bint** (girl)

  u   like the vowel in 'put' or 'hood', as in <u>**sh**</u>**uft** (I saw)

  and five long ones:

  aa   like a longer version of the vowel in 'met', as in **haat** (bring)

  ii   like the vowel in 'keen', as in **miin?** (who?)

  uu   like the vowel in 'food', as in **nuur** (light)

  oo   like the vowel in 'home', except the lips are rounder and tenser, as in **yoom** (day)

  ee   like the vowel in 'may' or 'lane', but with the lips more widely and tensely spread, as in **feen?** (where?)

- The consonants

  The sounds represented by b, d, f, g, h, j, k, l, m, n, s, t, v, w, y, z are virtually identical to their English counterparts.

  <u>**sh**</u>   (underlined) represents the sound you find in 'shoot' or 'shop' and not the one in 'mishap'; eg <u>**sh**</u>**aay** (tea)

  r   a 'rolled' r, made by vibrating the tip of the tongue behind the teeth, as in **wara** (behind)

  S, T, D, Z represent 'heavy' or 'thick' versions of s, t, d, and z. They are pronounced with the muscles of the lips and the tongue very lax and loose, and can affect adjacent vowels, particularly aa, which is then pronounced more like the vowel in 'half'. Listen on the cassette to the difference in both the initial consonant and vowel in:

saami *(man's name)* and **Saafi** (pure)
taani (second) and **Taalib** (student)

<u>kh</u> (underlined) like the final sound in Scottish 'loch', as in **<u>kh</u>amsa** (five)

<u>gh</u> (underlined) like the French 'r' sound (like a very brief gargle!), as in **<u>gh</u>aali** (expensive)

indicates a glottal stop, which you find a lot in Cockney English replacing a 't', as in 'bu'er' or 'Sco'land'. In Arabic it is a sound in its own right, and not an indication that something has been omitted. Eg **ma'aas** (size)

q as in **ilqaahira** (Cairo) is similar to a 'k' sound, but produced further back, in about the same place as **<u>gh</u>**. It has the same effect on adjacent vowels as the 'thick' consonants.

H represents a very aspirated 'h'. You can achieve it by pretending you have drunk something very hot, breathing out heavily over the back of your tongue. When you make this sound, you should be able to feel the friction at the back of your throat. Eg **Haaga** (thing)

ع is an unfamiliar sound in English. It is somewhere between the glottal stop and the <u>gh</u> in <u>gh</u>aali, and is made with the whole of the tongue as far back as possible in the throat; as in ع**ala** (on)

Consonants, like vowels, may be long; we have indicated this by doubling the letter. You must pronounce these consonants as doubles, ie as in English 'smalllad' or 'commonname'.

Sala (prayer) **Salla** (he prayed)
ana (I) **fanni** (artistic)

The definite article (the) is **il-** and is joined to the noun:

kart (a card) **ilkart** (the card)

But when the noun begins with any of the following consonants:

t d n s z sh r T D S Z

the 'l' disappears and the first consonant is doubled and pronounced long:

nuur (light)   **innuur** (the light)
raagil (a man) **irraagil** (the man)

In short words like **fi** (at, in), **wi** (and), **li** (to, for), the 'i' often disappears when another vowel precedes or follows:

talaata w nuSS (three and a half)
ilwalad w ilbint (the boy and the girl)
f ilqaahira (in Cairo)

If a word ends in two consonants and the next word begins with one, Egyptians often put in a short 'helping' vowel, to avoid the combination of three consonants in a row, which they find difficult. This is shown in the transcripts of the recorded conversations by an italic *i*, eg **nuSS*i* kiilu** (half a kilo).

It's important to stress a word in the right place; if the final vowel is long, it is stressed:

maZb**uu**T   bar**ii**d

Otherwise the last syllable but one normally carries the stress:

mud**a**rris   mudarr**i**sa

The few exceptions to the above are shown with a written accent, like this:

d**á**raga   s**á**laTa

Finally, the best way of acquiring a reasonable pronunciation is to imitate the speakers in the programmes or the cassettes. You could also try saying aloud the key words at the beginning of each chapter, and then compare them with the native speaker's version. Best of all, of course, find an Egyptian to help you!

While you should try to be as accurate as possible in pronounciation, Arabic speakers are not only used to hearing a wide variety of accents from within the Arab world, they are also genuinely delighted to find a foreigner making an effort to speak Arabic.

Listen and repeat

The following word-list demonstrates the sounds of Arabic. The words are given at the start of Cassette 1.

Long vowels
haat	miin	yoom	feen	nuur

Thick consonants
saam Saam taab Taab daani Daani zaahir Zaahir

Other unfamiliar constants

r	raagil	bariid	kart
kh	khubz	khaalid	sukhna
gh	ghaali	baghdaad	ghani
q	qaasim	ilqaahira	qarya
k/q	kalb/qalb	kaam/qaam	
H	Haal	Hisaab	aHmad
h/H	haal/Haal	hadd/Hadd	
'	'ahwa	ba'shiish	la'
ع	عala	عaawiz	saعiid
'/ع	'amal/عamal	ma'aas/maعaad	'aal/عaal

Long consonants

sitta	iddiini	innuur
iTTaalib	issana	ishshanTa

Watch the stress

muhandis muhandisa	itfaDDal itfaDDali
Taalib Taaliba	kwayyis kwayyisa
Sughayyar Sughayyara	kallim kallimni

1 Meeting people

Key expressions

ahlan ahlan wa sahlan	hallo, nice to meet you
ahlan biik	*reply (to a man)*
ahlan biiki	*reply (to a woman)*
SabaaH ilkheer	good morning
SabaaH innuur	*reply*
misaa' ilkheer	good evening
misaa' innuur	*reply*
izzayyak?	how are you? (*to a man*)
izzayyik?	how are you? (*to a woman*)
ismak 'eeh?	what is your name? (*to a man*)
ismik 'eeh?	what is your name? (*to a woman*)
ismi shiriif	my name is shiriif
ana min landan	I am from London
ana muhandis	I am an engineer
maɛa ssalaama	goodbye
ashuufak imta?	when will I see you? (*to a man*)
ashuufik imta?	when will I see you? (*to a woman*)

Conversations

1 Hello! How are you?

Two girls meet ...

zeenab	aah! naahid! izzayyik?
naahid	ilHamdu lillaah, kwayyisa. w inti, izzayyik?
zeenab	ana kwayyisa, ilHamdu lillaah.

In the morning two boys meet ...

Taari'	heey! SabaaH ilkheer!

shiriif	SabaaH innuur ya Taari'! izzayyak?
Taari'	ilHamdu lillaah, kwayyis. w izzayyak inta?
shiriif	ilHamdu lillaah, kwayyis.

In the evening ...

Taari'	heey! misaa' ilkheer.
muudi	misaa' innuur.
Taari'	izzayyak ya muudi?
muudi	izzayyak inta?
Taari'	ilHamdu lillaah, kwayyis, w inta?
muudi	ilHamdu lillaah, kwayyis.

ismi Taari'. w inti ?

ismi zeenab.

2 What's your name ...?

mu'nis	ahlan.
'inaas	ahlan biik.
mu'nis	inti ismik 'eeh?
'inaas	ana ismi 'inaas. w inta?
mu'nis	ismi mu'nis.

3 ...and where are you from?

sanaa'	ismak 'eeh?
shiriif	ismi shiriif. w inti ismik 'eeh?
sanaa'	ana ismi sanaa'.

shiriif	inti mineen, ya sanaa'?
sanaa'	ana min hina, min maSr. w inta
	mineen?
shiriif	ana min buur saƐiid.
sanaa'	ahlan wa sahlan.
shiriif	ahlan biiki.

Taari' meets people from around the Arab world.

Taari'	misaa' il<u>kh</u>eer.
Man	misaa' innuur.
Taari'	inta mineen min faDlak?
Man	ana min issudaan, min il<u>kh</u>artuum.
Man	...ana min iSSumaal.
Man	...ana min issuƐudiyya.
Man	...ana min ilqaahira.
Man	...ana min 'aSwaan.
Man	...ana min nuuba.

4 What do you do ...?

Man	ana muhandis. w inta?
Man	ana mudiir bank.
Woman	ana mudarrisa. w inti?
Woman	ana duktuura.
Man	ana Taalib. w inta?
Man	ana Taalib kamaan.

5 Saying goodbye ...

zeenab and her friend arrange to meet the next day.

zeenab	a<u>sh</u>uufik imta?
Friend	a<u>sh</u>uufik bukra, in <u>sh</u>a'allaah.
zeenab	bukra... hina?
Friend	'aywa, hina.
zeenab	maƐa ssalaama.
Friend	maƐa ssalaama.

Vocabulary

ana *I*
inta *you* (m)
inti *you* (f)
huwwa *he*
hiyya *she*
'aywa *yes*
la' *no*
wi *and*
kamaan *also*
ilHamdu lillaah *fine*
kwayyis *fine, well*
bi kheer *fine, well*
'eeh? *what?*
mineen? *where from?*
imta? *when?*
min *from*
hina *here*
maSr *Egypt, Cairo*
  (see p19)

buur saƐiid *Port Said*
'aSwaan *Aswan*
nuuba *Nubia (S. Egypt)*
iSSumaal *Somalia*
issudaan *Sudan*
issuƐudiyya *Saudi Arabia*
ilkhartuum *Khartoum*
ism *name*
ya   used before person's
  name (see p17)
muhandis *engineer*
mudiir bank *bank manager*
mudarrisa *teacher* (f)
duktuura *doctor* (f)
Taalib *student*
ashuufik *I'll see you*
  (to a woman)
bukra *tomorrow*
in sha'allaah *God willing,*
  I hope so

Explanations

Arabic is rich in elaborate greetings, often with religious overtones. Here are a few of the commonest.

● Hello

   ahlan or **ahlan wa sahlan**
   Reply:
   ahlan or **ahlan biik** (to a man)
   ahlan biiki (to a woman)

● Good morning

   SabaaH ilkheer (*lit* morning of goodness)
   Reply:
   SabaaH ilkheer or **SabaaH innuur** (*lit* morning of light)
   'Morning' lasts till lunchtime, which may be at two or three o'clock.

● Good evening

   misaa' ilkheer
   Reply:
   misaa' ilkheer or **misaa' innuur**

● When talking directly to someone or calling them, you usually put **ya** in front of their name: **ahlan, ya huda**.

● How are you?

   izzayyak? (to a man)
   izzayyik? (to a woman)
   To be more emphatic, you can add the pronoun 'you' - **inta** to a man, **inti** to a woman:
   izzayyak inta?   izzayyik inti?

● **wi** means 'and'. Notice the 'i' disappears before another vowel: **w inta, izzayyak?**

- I'm fine ...

  kwayyis (if you're a man)
  kwayyisa (if you're a woman)
  Notice **-a** is usually added to adjectives and
  nouns to make them feminine.
  bi kheer is another way of saying 'fine', but it
  never changes.
  Almost always people add **ilHamdu lillaah** (*lit*
  praise be to God). In fact, it is often used alone
  without **kwayyis** or **bi kheer**.
  izzayyak? ilHamdu lillaah

- 'I' is **ana**.

  In a sentence like **ana kwayyisa** (I'm fine), **inta
  mineen?** (where are you from?) or **zeenab min
  maSr** (zeenab is from Egypt), there is no word
  equivalent to 'am', 'are' or 'is'.

- 'Name' is **ism**

  If you want to say 'my name' you add **-i**: **ismi
  shiriif**.
  'Your *(m)* name' is **ismak**.
  'Your *(f)* name' is **ismik**.

- 'What?' is **'eeh?** To ask someone their name:
  (to a woman) **ismik** | **'eeh?**
     (to a man) **ismak** |
  (*lit* your name is what?)
  Again, the pronouns 'I' and 'you' are often
  added for emphasis:
  inta ismak 'eeh? ana ismi shiriif

- 'Where from?' is **mineen?** Like **'eeh,** this follows
  the subject:
  inta mineen? huda mineen?
  To reply you use **min** (from) with the name of a
  place:
  ana min landan. huda min maSr.

- 'He' is **huwwa**. 'She' is **hiyya**.
  When using the feminine pronouns **hiyya** or **inti**, the noun or adjective must be feminine:
  huwwa duktuur he's a doctor
  hiyya duktuura she's a doctor
  huwwa kwayyis he's fine
  hiyya kwayyisa she's fine
  There's often a shift in stress when an 'a' is added:
  mudarris, mudarrisa; muhandis, muhandisa

- To say goodbye ...
  maᶜa ssalaama (with peace). The reply is the same.

- 'When?' is **imta?** To ask 'When shall I see you?':
  (to a woman) **ashuufik** │ **imta?**
  (to a man) **ashuufak** │

  You will hear **in sha'allaah** (God willing) all the time; it almost automatically follows any reference to future plans (as in the last conversation: **ashuufik bukra, in sha'allaah** - 'I'll see you tomorrow, I hope'). With the right kind of slightly doubtful intonation, it can even be a polite way of saying no.

Additional vocabulary

briTanya *Britain*	ostralya *Australia*
amriika *America*	ilhind *India*
ingiltira *England*	bakistaan *Pakistan*
iskotlanda *Scotland*	ilyabaan *Japan*
airlanda *Ireland*	iSSiin *China*
weelz *Wales*	rusya *Russia*
kánada *Canada*	baraziil *Brazil*

See map on p4 for the names of all the Arab countries.
NB **maSr** is 'Egypt', but is also used colloquially for 'Cairo'. The formal name for Cairo is **ilqaahira**.

mudarris/mudarrisa	*teacher*
duktuur/duktuura	*doctor*
Taalib/Taaliba	*student*
muhandis/muhandisa	*engineer*
mudiir/mudiira	*manager, director*
SaHafi/SaHafiyya	*journalist*
khabiir/khabiira	*expert, consultant*
sikirteer/sikirteera	*secretary*
ɛaamil/ɛaamila	*worker*
sitt/ beet	*housewife*
raagil 'aɛmaal	*businessman*
issalaamu ɛaleekum	(lit *Peace be upon you* - at any time of day)
ɛaleekum issalaam	Reply
marHaba	*Welcome*
marHaba biik	Reply (to a man)
marHaba biiki	Reply (to a woman)
keef Haalak?	*How are you?* (to a man)
keef Haalik?	*How are you?* (to a woman)
tiSbaH ɛala <u>kh</u>eer	*Good night* (to a man)
tiSbaHi ɛala kheer	*Good night* (to a woman)

Exercises

---

1 Pretend your name is John, and you are from England (**ingiltira**). Now answer the following questions:

a inta mineen?
b ismak 'eeh?

2 Answer questions **a** and **b** again. This time you are Taari', from Cairo.

3 What time of day would you greet people in the following way:

a misaa' ilkheer
b SabaaH ilkheer
c ahlan wa sahlan

4 Give appropriate replies to **3a**, **b**, and **c**.

5 You are meeting <u>shiriif</u> for the first time.
a Say hallo and ask him his name.
b Now ask him where he's from.

6 You are meeting naahid for the first time.
a Say hallo and ask her her name.
b Now ask her where she is from.

7 You meet mu'nis, whom you already know.
a Say 'Good morning, mu'nis'.
b Ask him how he is.
c Ask him when you'll see him.
d When he suggests tomorrow, say 'I hope so'.

Mohamed Ali Mosque, Cairo

2 Food and drink

Key expressions

fiih ɛaSiir?	is there any juice?
mafii<u>sh</u> biira hina	there's no beer here
ɛandak | 'eeh?	what have you *(m)* got?
ɛandik |	what have you *(f)* got?
ilHisaab, min faDlak	the bill, please
ana | ɛaawiz | | want	I *(m)* | want
| ɛawza |	I *(f)* | want
iddiini ...	give me ...
ti<u>sh</u>rab | 'eeh?	what will you *(m)* drink?
ti<u>sh</u>rabi |	what will you *(f)* drink?
<u>sh</u>ukran	thank you
ɛafwan; ilɛafw	not at all

Conversations

1 Something to drink ...

Waiter	ti<u>sh</u>rab 'eeh?
Taari'	a<u>sh</u>rab <u>sh</u>aay.
Waiter	HaaDir.
Taari'	<u>sh</u>ukran.

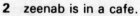

2 zeenab is in a cafe.

Waiter	ti<u>sh</u>rabi 'eeh?
zeenab	ɛandak 'eeh?
Waiter	<u>sh</u>aay walla 'ahwa walla Haaga saɛa?
zeenab	'ahwa maZbuuT, min faDlak.
Waiter	HaaDir.

3 Two coffees, a tea and water pipe.

Waiter	SabaaH ilkheer. ayyi khidma?
Taari'	SabaaH innuur. iddiini itneen 'ahwa w waaHid shaay.
Waiter	(*shouting out to kitchen*) itneen 'ahwa, waaHid shaay!
Cook	HaaDir.
Taari'	(*calling after the waiter*) wi shiisha, min faDlak!

4 Many cafes don't sell alcoholic drinks ...

Taari'	ɛandak biira min faDlak?
Waiter	mafiish biira hina, ya beeh.
Taari'	shukran.
Waiter	ilɛafw, ya beeh.

5 ..but some of them do.

Taari'	ɛandak biira?
Waiter	'aywa, ɛandi biira.
Taari'	iddiini talaata biira min faDlak.
Waiter	HàaDir.
Taari'	(*later*) ilHisaab, min faDlak.
Waiter	'aywa.

6 Asking what juices there are.

zeenab	SabaaH ilkheer.
Waiter	SabaaH innuur.
zeenab	ɛandak ɛaSiir 'eeh, min faDlak?
Waiter	fiih ɛaSiir burTu'aan, fiih ɛaSiir gawaafa, fiih ɛaSiir manga, fiih ɛaSiir farawla, fiih ɛaSiir lamuun.
zeenab	ɛandak grepfruut?
Waiter	la', ɛaSiir grepfruut mafiish.
zeenab	waaHid gawaafa, min faDlak.
Waiter	HaaDir.

7 Asking what sandwiches they have ...

zeenab	SabaaH ilkheer.
Girl	SabaaH innuur.

zeenab	ɛandik sandwitshaat 'eeh, min faDlik?
Girl	ɛandi fuul wi Taɛmiyya w beeD wi kufta w kibda.
zeenab	ɛandik gibna?
Girl	la', maɛandiish gibna.
zeenab	waaHid Taɛmiyya min faDlik.
Girl	HaaDir.

8 ... and what soup they have.

Taari'	misaa' ilkheer.
Waiter	misaa' innuur.
Taari'	fiih shurba?
Waiter	'aywa, y afandim. fiih shurba.
Taari'	shurbit 'eeh?
Waiter	fiih shurbit khuDaar, shurbit baSal.
Taari'	iddiini shurbit baSal, min faDlak.
Waiter	HaaDir.

9 Ordering a complete meal.

kamaal	misaa' ilkheer.
Waiter	misaa' innuur, ahlan wa sahlan.
kamaal	shukran. ilminyu min faDlak.
Waiter	itfaDDal. itfaDDali ya madaam.
huda/kamaal	shukran.
huda	min faDlak, ɛawza waaHid samak mashwi, wi waaHid baTaaTis, wi waaHid sabaanikh.
kamaal	ɛaawiz waaHid ruzz wi waaHid firaakh wi waaHid bisilla, min faDlak.
Waiter	Haaga kamaan?
kamaal	'aywa, itneen mayya maɛdaniyya min faDlak.
Waiter	HaaDir.
Later	
kamaal	ilHisaab min faDlak.
Waiter	itfaDDal.
kamaal	itfaDDal ... da ɛalashaanak.
Waiter	shukran. maɛa ssalaama.

Vocabulary

waaHid *one*
itneen *two*
talaata *three*
arba9a *four*
khamsa *five*
burTu'aan *orange*
gawaafa *guava*
manga *mango*
farawla *strawberry*
lamuun *lemon*
grepfruut *grapefruit*
minyu *menu*
sandwitsh *sandwich*
shurba *soup*
samak *fish*
firaakh *chicken*
mashwi *grilled*
ruzz *rice*
khuDaar *vegetables*
baTaaTis *potatoes*
bisilla *peas*
beeD *eggs*
fuul *cooked beans*
falaafil; taƐmiyya *deep-fried cakes of chick peas or beans*
kufta *meat balls*
kibda *liver*
gibna *cheese*
baSal *onion*
ƐaSiir *juice*

mayya (maƐdaniyya) *(mineral) water*
biira *beer*
'ahwa *coffee*
shaay *tea*
shiisha *hubble bubble*
Haaga *thing, something*
Haaga sa'Ɛa *something cold*
maZbuuT *medium sweet*
ashrab *I drink*
tishrab *you (m) drink*
tishrabi *you (f) drink*
Ɛandak? *do you (m) have?*
mafiish *there isn't/aren't*
maƐandiish *I haven't*
ya beeh *sir*
y afandim *sir*
ya madaam *madam*
... walla ... *... or ...*
ayyi khidma *can I help you?/don't mention it (lit any service)*
HaaDir *certainly, at once*
itfaDDal *here you (m) are*
itfaDDali *here you (f) are*
da Ɛalashaanak *that's for you (when tipping a man)*

Explanations

● 'Have'

is expressed not by a verb but by means of
Ɛand- (with), plus a personal ending, 'me', 'you'
etc:

I have Ɛandi

you have Ɛandak *(m)*
          Ɛandik *(f)*

eg ʕandak 'eeh? what have you (m) got?
ʕandak biira? do you have (any) beer?

- The same endings can be added to ʕalashaan (for):
  da ʕalashaanak 'that's for *you*' (*eg when giving a tip*). To a woman: da ʕalashaanik

- 'There is/are...' is the invariable **fiih**:
  fiih ʕaSiir? is there (any) juice?
  fiih biira? is there (any) beer?
  'aywa, fiih yes, there is

- 'Not'
  Both **fiih** and **ʕand-** are made negative by adding ma.....**sh**:
  ʕandi I have; maʕandiish I haven't
  fiih there is; mafiish there isn't
  mafiish biira hina there's no beer here

- 'I want' is:
  ana ʕaawiz (or ʕaayiz) (if you're a man)
  ana ʕawza (or ʕayza) (if you're a woman)
  ʕaawiz is an adjective and so takes the feminine -a ending:
  eg hiyya ʕawza ʕaSiir she wants (some) juice

- **ashrab** I drink
  tishrab you *(m)* drink
  tishrabi you *(f)* drink
  When inviting someone to have a drink, say **tishrab 'eeh?** (to a man) or **tishrabi 'eeh?** (to a woman).

- You often add **-i** for the feminine:
  itfaDDal, itfaDDali (*lit* kindly accept...)
  This is used in any situation where you are offering something politely to somebody. It can

mean 'have a seat', 'please come in', 'have a drink', 'please join us' and so on.

● Noun + noun

As in English, two nouns can come together, one modifying the other: eg ɛaSiir lamuun (lemon juice), **mudiir bank** (bank manager). But notice the order is reversed in Arabic. If the first noun ends in the feminine -**a**, this ending changes to -**it** when another noun follows: **shurba** soup, *but* **shurbit baSal** onion soup
                    shurbit 'eeh? what soup?

● More than one

A common way of forming the plural is by adding -**aat**, as in **sandwitsh, sandwitshaat**. The numbers from one to five are given in the vocabulary on page 25; when ordering food and drink, a number is used with the singular noun: **itneen biira** two beers
itneen 'ahwa two coffees

● 'The'

Put **il**- before the noun:
Hisaab a bill; **ilHisaab** the bill
The 'l' of il in some cases forms a long consonant with the following sound: **issabaanikh** - the spinach' (*not* ilsabaanikh). (See Guide to pronunciation, p11).

● Polite terms of address vary from country to country. In Egypt, some of the commonest, to a man, are **ya beeh** and **y afandim**; to a woman, **ya madaam**.

● If you are inviting someone to make a choice, the equivalent of '...or...?' is ...**walla**...?:
'ahwa walla shaay? coffee or tea?

Worth knowing

Besides eating in restaurants and hotels, you may want to eat at a snack bar, where you'll find sandwiches, often made with flat pitta-type bread (**khubz baladi**, or 'local bread') fried snacks like falaafil, kebab, and fresh fruit juice.
Fast food eating places are increasingly popular in the Middle East, and range from traditional roadside kiosks to the modern international food chains.

In some cake shops you can eat a delicious pastry on the spot with a glass of iced water, or take it with you.

Street cafes are for sipping tea, coffee and soft drinks at your leisure; in areas not much visited by tourists they tend to be patronised mainly by men. There the **shiisha** - the water pipe or 'hubble bubble' - is a common sight.

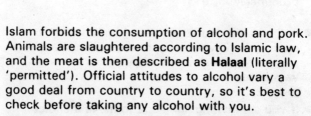

Islam forbids the consumption of alcohol and pork. Animals are slaughtered according to Islamic law, and the meat is then described as **Halaal** (literally 'permitted'). Official attitudes to alcohol vary a good deal from country to country, so it's best to check before taking any alcohol with you.

Ramadan is the month when Moslems fast during the hours of daylight, so it is generally polite not to eat, drink or smoke in public places during these hours.

If you order tea or coffee in a cafe, it will usually be served black - the tea with lots of sugar. Traditional 'Turkish' coffee can be **maZbuuT** (medium sweet), **saada** (without sugar) or **sukkar ziyaada** (very sweet).

Additional vocabulary

'akl *food*
sukkar *sugar*
laban *milk*
|Haliib *milk*|
malH *salt*
filfil *pepper*
talg *ice*
khubz *bread*
mezza *hors d'oeuvres*
Hummus *chick peas (often served as a creamy dip)*
TiHiina *sesame seed paste*
sálaTa khaDra *mixed salad*
makaroona *macaroni (or other pasta)*
bidingaan *aubergines*

faSulya *butter beans*
TamaaTim *tomatoes*
gambari *prawns, shrimps*
laHm *meat*
Hamaam *pigeon*
*|dajaaj *chicken*|
gazar *carrots*
shawirma *spiced grilled meat*
nibiit *wine*
'izaaza *bottle*
aHmar *red*
abyaD *white*
aiskriim *ice-cream*
mooz *bananas*
tuffaaH *apples*
mishmish *apricots*
tiin *figs*

Traditional oriental pastries often made with honey and nuts include **ba'laawa, basbuusa, kunaafa,** and **'aTaayif** - all of which may be served **b il'ishTa** - with whipped cream.

* Words shown in square brackets are not Egyptian but are in common use in other parts of the Arab World.

Exercises

1 Ask a waiter politely (ie say 'please') for the following:

a an orange juice
b two beers
c a sandwich

d   a medium sweet coffee
e   vegetable soup
f   the bill

2   What would change if it were a waitress?

3   Ask whether the following are available, using **fiih**:

a   coffee
b   mango juice
c   onion soup
d   rice
e   sandwiches

4   Ask for the same items using ʕ**andak**.

5   Think of questions or comments which might have prompted the following replies:

a   'aywa, ʕandi sandwitshaat gibna.
b   la', mafiish nibiit hina.
c   la', maʕandiish mayya maʕdaniyya.
d   HaaDir....itfaDDal ilHisaab.
e   ʕafwan.

Using the additional vocabulary at the end of the chapter try ordering a really elaborate meal!

3 Shopping

Key expressions

---

bi kam?	how much?
i<u>shsh</u>anTa di	this/that bag
ilgamal da	this/that camel
(bi) ʕi<u>sh</u>riin gineeh	(for) twenty pounds
mumkin	possible
mi<u>sh</u> mumkin	not possible
mumkin a<u>sh</u>tiri?	can I buy?
mumkin a<u>sh</u>uufha?	can I see it *(f)*?
di'ii'a waHda	one moment
(ana) | 'aasif | 'asfa	(I'm) | sorry *(m)* | sorry *(f)*
ʕandak Sanf 'aHsan?	have you got a better kind?
ʕandak ma'aas 'akbar?	have you got a bigger size?
<u>gh</u>aali 'awi	very expensive
bi balaa<u>sh</u>	free *(lit* for nothing)

Conversations

---

1 Asking the price of a souvenir camel ...

Taari'	min faDlak, bi kam ilgamal da?
Shopkeeper	b itneen gineeh wi nuSS.
Taari'	bi kam?
Shopkeeper	itneen gineeh wi nuSS.
Taari'	w ilkibiir?
Shopkeeper	<u>kh</u>amsa gineeh.
Taari'	<u>sh</u>ukran.
Shopkeeper	ilʕafw.

2 ... a bag ...

Taari'	SabaaH ilkheer.
Shopkeeper	SabaaH innuur.
Taari'	bi kam ishshanTa di?
Shopkeeper	ɛishriin gineeh.
Taari'	wi di?
Shopkeeper	itnaashar gineeh.
Taari'	bi kam?
Shopkeeper	itnaashar gineeh.
Taari'	shukran.
Shopkeeper	ɛafwan.

3 ... and a galabiyya.

Taari'	bi kam ilgallabiyya di?
Shopkeeper	sabɛa gineeh wi nuSS.
Taari'	w ilHamra di?
Shopkeeper	w ilHamra di, bi tamanya gineeh.
Taari'	shukran.
Shopkeeper	ayyi khidma.

4 zeenab wants some postcards.

zeenab	ɛandak kart buSTaal, min faDlak?
Shopkeeper	'aywa, ɛandi. itfaDDali.
zeenab	bi kam ilkart?
Shopkeeper	bi ɛashar 'uruush.

zeenab	*(she chooses three)* talaata min faDlak.
Shopkeeper	talatiin 'irsh, min faDlik.
zeenab	Ɛandak TawaabiƐ, min faDlak?
Shopkeeper	la', 'aasif, maƐandiish.
zeenab	<u>sh</u>ukran ... itfaDDal gineeh.
Shopkeeper	itfaDDali <u>kh</u>amsiin, sittiin, sabƐiin.
zeenab	<u>sh</u>ukran.
Shopkeeper	maƐa ssalaama.
zeenab	maƐa ssalaama.

5 Can I buy stamps here?

Taari'	mumkin a<u>sh</u>tiri Tawaabiɛ hina?
Shopgirl	'aywa, mumkin.
Taari'	iddiini talat TawaabiƐ l ingiltira, min faDlik.
Shopgirl	HaaDir.

6 A film for the camera.

Taari'	mumkin a<u>sh</u>tiri film l ilkamera di?
Shopgirl	mumkin a<u>sh</u>uufha?
Taari'	*(handing it over)* itfaDDali.
Shopgirl	sitta w talatiin, walla arbaƐa w Ɛi<u>sh</u>riin Suura?
Taari'	sitta w talatiin mulawwan.
Shopgirl	HaaDir. di'ii'a waHda. *(she fetches a film)* itfaDDal. talaata gineeh wi <u>kh</u>amsa w sabƐiin 'ir<u>sh</u>.
Taari'	itfaDDali.
Shopgirl	<u>sh</u>ukran.
Taari'	<u>sh</u>ukran. maƐa ssalaama.
Shopgirl	maƐa ssalaama.

7 Sometimes you'll have to bargain ...

Customer	issalaamu Ɛaleekum.
Shopkeeper	Ɛaleekum issalaam.
Customer	min faDlak, bi kam i<u>shsh</u>anTa di?
Shopkeeper	bi tamanya w Ɛi<u>sh</u>riin gineeh.
Customer	la', mi<u>sh</u> mumkin. <u>gh</u>alya 'awi.

Shopkeeper	bi balaash ɛalashaanik ...
	ɛawzaaha bi kam?
Customer	bi ɛishriin gineeh.
Shopkeeper	la'! mumkin bi talaata w ɛishriin.
Customer	Tayyib. itfaDDal.
Shopkeeper	shukran. maɛa ssalaama.

8 ... or ask for a better kind ...

Customer	ɛandak Sanf 'aHsan?
Shopkeeper	'aywa, ɛandi. bass ghaali.
Customer	ɛandak Sanf 'aHsan?
Shopkeeper	la'. da 'aHsan Sanf.

9 ... or a larger size ...

Customer	ɛandak ma'aas 'akbar?
Shopkeeper	ɛandi. ma'aas kam?
Customer	itneen w arbiɛiin.

10 ... or something cheaper.

| Customer | fiih Haaga 'arkhaS? |
| Shopgirl | la', 'asfa, mafiish. |

Vocabulary

bi *for* (in prices), *with*	Suura (*pl* Suwar) *picture*
gallabiyya (*pl* -aat)	ghaali (*f* ghalya) *expensive*
galabiyya	li *to, for*
gineeh *pound*	'awi *very, too*
'irsh (*pl* 'uruush) *piastre*	ashtiri *I buy*
kart (*pl* kuruut) buSTaal	bass *but, only*
postcard	'aHsan *better, best*
Taabiɛ (*pl* Tawaabiɛ)	rikhiiS *cheap*
stamp	'arkhaS *cheaper, cheapest*
nuSS *half*	kibiir *big*
'aHmar (*f* Hamra) *red*	'akbar *bigger, biggest*
kámera *camera*	Sanf (*pl* 'aSnaaf) *kind,*
film (*pl* aflaam) *film*	*type*
mulawwan *coloured,*	ma'aas *size*
in colour	Tayyib ... *OK, well*
di'ii'a *minute, moment*	*now ...*

Numbers

6	sitta (*before plural noun* - sitt)		
7	sab£a (*before plural noun* - saba£)		
8	tamanya (*before plural noun* - taman)		
9	tis£a (*before plural noun* - tisa£)		
10	£áshara (*before plural noun* - £ashar)		

11	Hidaashar	16	sittaashar
12	itnaashar	17	saba£taashar
13	talattaashar	18	tamantaashar
14	arba£taashar	19	tisa£taashar
15	khamastaashar		

20	£ishriin	50	khamsiin	80	tamaniin
30	talatiin	60	sittiin	90	tis£iin
40	arbi£iin	70	sab£iin	100	miyya

NB As with 6-10 above, talaata becomes talat and arba£a, arba£ before a plural noun.

Explanations

● To ask the price of an object:

	ilgallabiyya?		the galabiyya?
bi kam	**ilgamal?**	how much is	the camel?
	ishshanTa?		the bag?

or: **ilgallabiyya bi kam?**

The answer will be:

	gineeh	£1
(bi)	itneen gineeh	£2
	khamsa gineeh	£5 and so on

● **kam?** alone is used before a noun to mean 'how many?' or 'how much?', referring to quantities. The noun is always *singular:*

kam kart? how many cards?
kam sandwitsh? how many sandwiches?
kam sukkar? how much sugar?

● Adjectives have to add an **-a** to agree with feminine pronouns:
ana/inta/huwwa kwayyis

ana/inti/hiyya kwayyisa

They also agree with feminine nouns.

ilgamal *(m)*	the camel
ilgamal kibiir	the camel is big
ishshanTa *(f)*	the bag
ishshanTa kibiira	the bag is big

Not all adjectives make the feminine like
kwayyisa. We show other types like this:

'aHmar *(f* Hamra) *red*
ghaali *(f* ghalya) *expensive*

● To say 'a big bag' or 'an expensive galabiyya':
shanTa kibiira
gallabiyya ghalya

● To say 'the big bag' or 'the expensive
galabiyya', add **il-** to the adjective as well as the
noun but remember the rules given on p11:
ishshanTa ilkibiira
ilgallabiyya ilghalya

● 'This' or 'that'
Make the noun definite (by putting **il-** first), then
add **da** to a masculine, **di** to a feminine noun:

ilgamal da	this/that camel
ilgallabiyya di	this/that galabiyya

If it's clear what you're talking about, **da** or **di**
can be used alone. So can any adjective:

da bi kam?	how much is that *(m)*?
di ghalya!	that *(f)* is expensive!
w ilkibiir	and the big one *(m)*?
w ilHamra?	and the red one *(f)*?

● To make a 'verbless' statement negative, add
mish as follows:

ana min landan	ana **mish** min landan
huwwa hina	huwwa **mish** hina
da ghaali	da **mish** ghaali

● One way of forming plurals is to add **-aat** (see p27):

sandwitsh   sandwitshaat

Often nothing is added, but the pattern of vowels in the word is rearranged (a bit like English 'mouse, mice').

kart (a card)   **kuruut** (cards)
'irsh (a piastre)   **'uruush** (piastres)

The pattern used for **Taabiξ** (a stamp) is **Tawaabiξ**.

There are about half a dozen major patterns (see Reference section p71-72). You can't necessarily predict the plural, so we give the main ones in the vocabulary lists like this:

film (*pl* **aflaam**)

● The numbers 1 - 5 were given on p25; 6 - 100 are given on p35.

waaHid (one) has the feminine form **waHda**. eg **di'ii'a waHda** one moment

To say '24', '35', etc, Arabic uses 'four and twenty', 'five and thirty' etc:

arbaξa w ξishriin: 24   **khamsa w talatiin**: 35

It's useful to divide the numbers into two sets: up to ten, and eleven upwards.
The numbers 2 - 10 are followed by a plural noun (*except* when ordering food and drink), and the final **-a** of the number is dropped:

talaata (on its own), *but*
talat Tawaabiξ   three stamps
ξashar 'uruush   ten piastres

Numbers from eleven upwards don't change and are followed by a *singular* noun:

talatiin 'irsh   thirty piastres
arbaξa w ξishriin Suura   twenty-four pictures

● Basic units of length and weight are invariable:

mitr   a metre
khamsa mitr   five metres

| kiilu | a kilo |
| sitta kiilu | six kilos |

The same applies to **gineeh** (the Egyptian £):

| gineeh | £1 |
| talaata gineeh | £3 |

● To say 'three and a half pounds' (*or* kilos *etc*) add **wi nuSS** after the noun:
  talaata gineeh wi nuSS; <u>kh</u>amsa kiilu wi nuSS etc

● To say 'a kilo of ...':

kiilu ilbur<u>T</u>u'aan	a kilo of oranges
nuSS kiilu issamak	half a kilo of fish
<u>kh</u>amsa kiilu ilba<u>T</u>aa<u>T</u>is	five kilos of potatoes

● **mumkin?** on its own means 'is it possible?', 'can I?', 'may I?', 'can we?', etc. The answer will be:
  '**aywa, mumkin** *or*
  la', mi<u>sh</u> mumkin

● To say 'I buy' and 'I see':

(ana) | **a<u>sh</u>tiri** | I buy
      | **a<u>sh</u>uuf** | I see

Add **mumkin** (is it possible?) to ask 'can I ...?':

mumkin | **a<u>sh</u>tiri?** | can I buy?
           | **a<u>sh</u>uuf?** | can I see?

● **-ha** ('it' for feminine nouns) or **-u** (for masculine nouns) may be added to the end:

| mumkin a<u>sh</u>uufha? | can I see it? (*eg* ilkámera) |
| mumkin a<u>sh</u>uufu? | can I see it? (*eg* ilgamal) |

NB In conversation 7, the shopkeeper says عawzaaha bi kam? (how much do you want to pay? - *lit* you want it for how much?) referring to i<u>shsh</u>an<u>T</u>a.

● Good, better, best ...

A special pattern is used for the comparative

and superlative of adjectives:

kibiir (big)	**'akbar** (bigger, biggest)
rikhiiS (cheap)	**'arkhaS** (cheaper, cheapest)
kitiir (a lot)	**'aktar** (more, most) etc

kwayyis (good) has the special comparative
'aHsan (better, best). So:

iSSanf da kwayyis	this kind is good
iSSanf da 'aHsan	that kind is better

The comparative *follows* the noun:

fiih Sanf 'aHsan?	is there a better kind?

The superlative *precedes* it:

da 'aHsan Sanf	that's the best kind

Fortunately these comparatives don't change in the feminine!

Additional vocabulary

fluus	*money*	
shibshib	*slippers*	
sandal (*pl* sanaadil)	*sandal*	
'amiiS (*pl* 'umSaan)	*shirt*	
fustaan (*pl* fasatiin)	*dress*	
'umaash	*material*	
'uTn	*cotton*	
Hariir	*silk*	
gild	*leather*	
'ufTaan (*pl* 'afaTiin)	*kaftan*	
banTaloon	*trousers*	

gazma (*pl* gizam)	*shoe*
kanaka	*coffee pot*
sanduu'	*box*
'alam	*pen, pencil*
Hilw	*beautiful, fine*
sigaara (*pl* sagaayir)	*cigarette*
kibriit	*matches*
raTl	*pound, half a kilo*
Sughayyar	*small*
'aSghar	*smaller, smallest*

Worth knowing

Currencies Besides the Egyptian gineeh, other currencies to be found in the Arab World are the riyaal, the dinaar, the liira and the dirham.

Bargaining

This is the accepted practice in the Middle East, at least when it comes to buying souvenirs. It is an amiable and often leisurely process - pursued over coffee or tea if a large item like a carpet is involved - but no offence is taken if you decide to 'think it over'. In countries where taxis don't have meters (or the meters tend not to work!), it's just as well to fix the price before you get in.

The galabiyya - a loose cotton gown ideal for hot climates - is the traditional form of dress for men in most Arab countries. It is usually simple in design -plain or striped - though more elaborate and brilliantly-coloured galabiyyas are produced for tourists. In Egypt, businessmen and office workers will probably wear European clothes rather than the galabiyya. In many other Arab countries though, it is the most usual form of dress for men of all classes.

The kaftan, a more formal version of the galabiyya, is often a heavier silk/cotton mixture - or wool for the winter - and is worn by both men and women.

Exercises

1 What is the difference in meaning between these four sentences?

a   <u>sh</u>anTa kibiira
b   i<u>shsh</u>anTa ilkibiira
c   i<u>shsh</u>anTa kibiira
d   i<u>shsh</u>anTa di kibiira

2 Ask a shopkeeper 'Have you got..., please?':

a any postcards
b any stamps
c a colour film
d a large bag
e a red galabiyya

3 Ask him if you can see the following:

a a galabiyya
b that camera
c a larger size
d a cheaper kind

4 Ask a shopkeeper the price of the following (checking your vocabulary from Chapter 2):

a a kilo of oranges
b half a kilo of lemons
c two kilos of bananas
d half a kilo of sugar

5 A shopkeeper gives the price of various items: tell him 'That is very expensive', using **da** or **di** as appropriate.

a ilgallabiyya bi talatiin gineeh.
b ilkart bi sittiin 'irsh.
c mitr il'umaash bi khamsa gineeh.
d ishshanTa bi itneen wi ɛishriin gineeh.

6 Ask him if there is:
a a bigger bag
b a smaller dress
c a cheaper camera
d a better kind

4 In the hotel

Key expressions

ɛandak 'ooDa?	do you have a room?
fiih mayya sukhna?	is there hot water?
ɛandi Hagz	I've got a reservation
kam leela?	how many nights?
bi kam illeela?	how much a night?
30 gineeh f ilyoom	£30 a day
'ooDa nimra ...	room number ...
issaaɛa kam?	what time is it?/at what time?
issaaɛa sabɛa	(it's) seven o'clock
mumkin adfaɛ ilHisaab?	can I pay the bill?
mumkin aɛmil tilifoon?	can I make a phone call?
mumkin aghayyar dolaraat?	can I change some dollars?
ɛala lyimiin/shshimaal	on the right/the left
imDi hina	sign here

Conversations

1 Taari' is booking a hotel room.

Taari'	misaa' ilkheer.
Clerk	misaa' innuur.
Taari'	ɛandak 'ooDa, min faDlak?
Clerk	di'ii'a waHda. *(checks in register)* 'aywa fiih. kam leela?
Taari'	leela waHda. fiih mayya sukhna?
Clerk	'aywa, wi fiih banyu wi tilifoon wi tilivizyoon f il'ooDa.
Taari'	bi kam il'ooDa?
Clerk	talatiin gineeh f ilyoom.
Taari'	iddiini 'ooDa, min faDlak.
Clerk	HaaDir.

2 zeenab wants a room for two nights.

zeenab	ɛandak 'ooDa, min faDlak?
Clerk	di'ii'a waHda. *(looks in register)* kam leela?
zeenab	lelteen, min faDlak.
Clerk	'aywa fiih.
zeenab	ɛayza 'ooDa bi Hammaam.
Clerk	fiih, mawguud.
zeenab	bi kam?
Clerk	tamanya w arbiɛiin gineeh.
zeenab	fiih maTɛam hina?
Clerk	'aywa, fiih maTɛam *(pointing)* hinaak.
zeenab	ilfiTaar issaaɛa kam?
Clerk	min sabɛa l ɛáshara.

3 If you already have a reservation ...

Taari'	ana ɛandi Hagz hina, min faDlak?.
Clerk	ismak 'eeh?
Taari'	Taari' ilbaguuri.
Clerk	'aywa, maZbuuT.
Taari'	shukran.
Clerk	da ilmuftaaH. il'ooDa suttumiyya w waaHid. il'asanSiir 'uddaam ɛala lyimiin.
Taari'	shukran. ilfiTaar issaaɛa kam?
Clerk	ilfiTaar min issaaɛa sabɛa l issaaɛa ɛáshara, hinaak f ilmaTɛam.
Taari'	shukran.
Clerk	ilɛafw.

4 Asking for the bill.

Taari'	mumkin adfaɛ ilHisaab, min faDlak?
Clerk	mumkin. di'ii'a waHda.
Taari'	shukran.

5 You may not always be lucky ...

Man	SabaaH ilkheer.
Clerk	SabaaH innuur.

Man	min faDlak, fiih 'ooDa faDya?
Clerk	Landak Hagz?
Man	la', maLandiish.
Clerk	'aasif, il'utiil malyaan.

6 And you may have to sign the register ...

Clerk	imDi hina min faDlak. iktib ismak w ism baladak.
Man	bi kulli suruur.
Clerk	itfaDDal ilmuftaaH. 'ooDa nimra miteen wi talatiin, f iddoor ittaani.
Man	shukran.

7 Can I call London?

Man	mumkin akallim landan min hina?
Clerk	mumkin. ittilifoon hina Lala shshimaal.
Man	shukran.

8 Changing money.

Man	mumkin aghayyar miyya w khamsiin dolaar?
Clerk	'aywa, TabLan. ilbasbuur, min faDlak.
Man	mumkin aghayyar shikaat siyaHiyya kamaan?
Clerk	'aywa, dolaraat kamaan?
Man	la', istirliini.

9 Making a phone call.

Man	mumkin aLmil tilifoon min hina?
Clerk	bi kulli suruur.
Man	*(dials)* ... 'alo? ... 'aywa, ya maHmuud! izzayyak inta? ... ilHamdu lillaah ... ana fi 'utiil shahriZaad, 'ooDa nimra miteen wi talatiin...Tayyib, bukra in sha'allaa h. tiSbaH Lala kheer.

Vocabulary

'ooDa (*pl* 'owaD) *room*
leela (*pl* layaali) *night*
sukhna *hot*
banyu *bath*
tilifoon *telephone*
tilivizyoon *television*
yoom (*pl* 'ayyaam) *day*
Hammaam *bathroom*
mawguud *there is*
maT𝒸am (*pl* maTaa𝒸im)
    restaurant
hinaak *there*
fiTaar *breakfast*
saa𝒸a *hour, time*
Hagz *reservation*
maZbuuT *right, exact*
muftaaH *key*
'asanSiir *lift*
'uddaam *opposite, in front*
𝒸ala *on*
yimiin *right*
shimaal *left*
adfa𝒸 *I pay*
faaDi (*f* faDya) *empty, free*

malyaan *full*
iktib *write*
imDi *sign*
balad *town, country*
nimra *number*
door *floor*
taani (*f* tanya) *second*
akallim *I speak to*
aghayyar *I change*
dolaar (*pl* dolaraat) *dollar*
Tab𝒸an *of course*
basbuur *passport*
shiik (*pl* -aat) siyaHiyya
    travellers cheque
istirliini *sterling*
a𝒸mil tilifoon *I make a
    phone call*
bi kulli suruur *certainly* (lit
    with all pleasure)
tiSbaH(i) 𝒸ala kheer *good
    night*
siriir *bed*
'aakul *I eat*
dushsh *shower*

Explanations

● To ask for a room:
  𝒸andak 'ooDa?

  To specify:

	Hammaam	bathroom
'ooDa bi	dushsh	shower
	mayya sukhna	hot water
	sirireen	two beds

  To say you've got a reservation:
  (ana) 𝒸andi Hagz

  You'll be told the price per day:

  | 𝒸ishriin | |
  | talatiin | gineeh f ilyoom |

- One ...

  waaHid *(m)* **waHda** *(f)*
  eg **yoom waaHid   leela waHda**

- Two ...

  itneen gineeh   £2
  itneen biira   two beers
  But most nouns have a special 'dual' form in
  which **-een** is added to the singular:
  yoom day   **yomeen** two days
  siriir bed   **sirireen** two beds
  If the noun is feminine, drop the **-a** and add
  -teen:
  leela night   **lelteen** two nights
  di'ii'a moment   **di'i'teen** two moments
  The dual of 'hundred' (**miyya**) is **miteen**.

- Hundreds

  On p76 of the reference section, you will find
  the forms taken by numbers 3 - 9 when they
  precede 'hundred'. In the hotel (conversation 3)
  the clerk says **suttumiyya** (six hundred).

- To ask the time:

  issaaƐa kam? (*lit* the hour how much?) has
  two meanings: 'what time is it?' and 'at what
  time?'
  To ask 'what time is ...?':
  ilfiTaar issaaƐa kam?   what time is breakfast?

- To tell the time:

issaaƐa	talaata	(it's)	three o'clock
	<u>kh</u>amsa		five o'clock
	sitta w nuSS		half past six

  To say 'from ... to ...':
  min issaaƐa sabƐa **l** issaaƐa Ɛashara

● Directions
  <u>(ish)shimaal</u>   (the) left
    (il)yimiin   (the) right
  They often come after ξala ('on'):

  ξala | **lyimiin**
       | **shshimaal**

● **'uddaam** (in front, opposite)
  It can be used on its own or take one of the
  pronouns:
  'uddaamak   in front of you *(m)*
  'uddaamik   in front of you *(f)*
  'uddaamha   in front of her

● Verbs
  More examples of 'I ...'

  (ana) | **adfaξ**   pay
        | **aakul**   eat
        | **aghayyar** change
        | **aξmil**   make, do
        | **akallim**   call (*lit* speak to)

  The above are all in the first person (I) and so all
  begin with **a-**. To make the second person (you),
  change the **a-** to **ti-**:
  tishrab 'eeh?   what are you drinking?

  mumkin | **tidfaξ?**   can you pay?
         | **tighayyar?**   can you change?

  NB mumkin **taakul** hina   you can eat here

  These are used when talking to a man. If talking
  to a woman, add a final **-i**:
  tishrabi 'eeh?

  mumkin | **tidfaξi?**
         | **tighayyari?**

  NB mumkin **takli** hina

  To tell someone to do something (the
  'imperative'), the initial **t-** is dropped:
  iktib (ismak)   write (your name) *(to a man)*
  iktibi (ismik) write (your name) *(to a woman)*

iddiini (give me) is another imperative of this kind.

- Polite phrases

    Apart from the phrases you are now familiar with, like **min faDlak** (please), **shukran** (thank you) and so on, you will also hear **bi kulli suruur** (certainly) - an even politer version of **HaaDir!**

    In conversation 9, Taari' says **tiSbaH ɛala kheer** (good night), which shows he's speaking to a man. To a woman, he'd have said **tiSbaHi ɛala kheer**. It literally means 'may the morning find you well'.

Additional vocabulary

ghurfa *room*	shaghghaal *working*
gawaaz issafar *passport*	mish shaghghaal *not working*
fuuTa (*pl* fuwaT) *towel*	b ilfiTaar *including breakfast*
niDiif *clean*	il'ooDa b ilfiTaar *bed and*
wisikh *dirty*	*breakfast*
haadi *quiet*	istiqbaal *reception*
dawsha *noise*	doorit mayya *lavatory*
ɛaTlaan *out of order, not*	twalett *lavatory*
working	takyiif hawa *air conditioning*
ittilifoon ɛaTlaan *the phone's*	khidma *service*
not working	ɛáshara f ilmiyya *10%*

Worth knowing

Information on accommodation, including up-to-date lists of hotels of various categories, can usually be obtained from the National Tourist Office of the country you are going to visit. This may not include much on the cheaper end of the market; if you want to live really simply, ask around on your arrival. Taxi drivers in the Middle East, as elsewhere, are usually invaluable sources of information.

Exercises

1 You are booking into a hotel; check whether there is:

a a bathroom
b a shower
c a telephone
d hot water

2 Now complain that the first three are not working (ɛaTlaan) and there's no hot water!

3 Ask whether you can:

a pay the bill
b make a phone call
c change some dollars

4 You want a single room for two nights; fill in your part of the conversation that follows, remembering to ask how much it costs!

Clerk	SabaaH ilkheer.
You	…
Clerk	ayyi khidma?
You	…
Clerk	'aywa, fiih. bi siriir waaHid walla bi sirireen?
You	…
Clerk	kam leela?
You	…
Clerk	fiih 'ooDa Hilwa f iddoor ittaani. itfaDDal ilmuftaaH.
You	…
Clerk	ɛishriin gineeh bass.

5 Out and about

Key expressions

il'utiil feen? feen il'utiil?	where is the hotel?
'awwil | shaariɛ taani |	first | street second |
'urayyib (min hina)	near (here)
bi9iid (min hina)	far (from here)
laazim taakhud taksi	you (m) must take a taxi
ɛaawiz aruuH ilharam	I want to go to the pyramids
shuwayya	a little, quite
kitiir	a lot
tazkara l iskindriyya	a ticket to Alexandria
dáraga | 'uula tanya	first | class second |
raayiH/raayiH gayy	single/return
raSiif nimra kam?	which platform?
feen 'a'rab 'agzakhaana?	where's the nearest chemist's?
imshi ɛala Tool	go straight on
da 'aTr iskindriyya?	is this the Alexandria train?

Conversations

1 Asking for a free map of the town.

Taari'	min faDlak?
Clerk	'aywa?
Taari'	ɛandak khariiTa l ilqaahira?
Clerk	'aywa.
Taari'	mumkin aakhud waHda?
Clerk	itfaDDal.
Taari'	shukran.
Clerk	ɛafwan.

2 Asking your way to Liberation Square.

Taari'	min faDlik, feen midaan ittaHriir?
Passerby	'awwil shaari£ ... *(correcting herself)* la', taani shaari£ £ala lyimiin.
Taari'	shukran.
Passerby	£afwan.

3 Is Khan El Khalili nearby?

Taari'	min faDlak, khan ilkhaliili 'urayyib min hina?
Passerby	la', bi£iid shuwayya. laazim taakhud taksi.
Taari'	shukran.
Passerby	£afwan.

4 Where is the nearest chemist's?

Tourist	min faDlak, feen 'a'rab 'agzakhaana?
Passerby	'awwil shaari£ £ala shshimaal.
Tourist	shukran.

5 Calling a taxi ...

mu'nis	taksi! taksi! £aawiz aruuH ilharam.
Driver	bi khamsa gineeh.
mu'nis	khamsa gineeh? kitiir! arba£a?
Driver	mumkin. itfaDDal.
mu'nis	shukran

6 ... and directing the taxi driver.

Driver	feen il'utiil?
mu'nis	imshi £ala Tool ...
Driver	*(drives on)* wi dilwa'ti?
mu'nis	shimaal hina ...
Driver	shimaal feen? shimaal hina?
mu'nis	'aywa. wi ba£deen taani shaari£ £ala lyimin.
Driver	hina?
mu'nis	'aywa. shukran.
Driver	il£afw.

7 Finding out about planes to Aswan.

Taari	misaa' il<u>kh</u>eer.
Assistant	misaa' innuur.
Taari'	ana ɛaayiz aruuH 'aSwaan.
Assistant	imta?
Taari'	baɛd bukra.
Assistant	baɛd bukra? litneen.
Taari'	'aywa.
Assistant	di'ii'a waHda. *(looking in timetable)* fiih Tayyaara issaaɛa tamanya wi <u>kh</u>amsa w arbiɛiin iSSubH, wi Tayyaara issaa9a itnaa<u>sh</u>ar wi nuSS iDDuhr.
Taari'	<u>sh</u>ukran. bi kam ittazkara?
Assistant	raayiH walla raayiH gayy?
Taari'	raayiH gayy.
Assistant	raayiH gayy? sabɛa w arbiɛiin gineeh.

8 Buying a train ticket.

Taari'	tazkara l iskindriyya min faDlak.
Clerk	dáraga 'uula walla dáraga tanya?
Taari'	dáraga 'uula.
Clerk	dáraga 'uula tamanha <u>kh</u>amsa gineeh.
Taari'	*(giving him the money)* itfaDDal. raSiif nimra kam?
Clerk	raSiif nimra arbaɛa.
Taari'	<u>sh</u>ukran.
Clerk	ɛafwan.

9 Checking that it's the right train.

Taari'	min faDlak?
Passerby	'aywa?
Taari'	da 'aTr iskindriyya?
Passerby	'aywa. da 'aTr iskindriyya.
Taari'	<u>sh</u>ukran.
Passerby	ɛafwan.

10 zeenab is going to the Egyptian museum in Cairo.

zeenab	min faDlak!
Passerby	'aywa?
zeenab	ilmatHaf feen?
Passerby	imshi Cala Tool, wi taani shaariC Cala lyimiin.
zeenab	shukran.
Passerby	Cafwan.
Later	
zeenab	bi kam ittazkara, min faDlak?
Attendant	tazkara bi talaata gineeh.
zeenab	iddiini tazkarteen.
Attendant	itneen ... sitta gineeh.

Vocabulary

khariiTa (l ilqaahira) map (of Cairo)
midaan square
midaan ittaHriir Liberation Square
'awwil (f 'uula) first
shaariC (pl shawaariC) street
khan ilkhaliili Khan El Khalili (bazaar area of Cairo)
laazim (it is) necessary
taksi (pl taksiyyaat) taxi
'a'rab nearest
'agzakhaana chemist's
aruuH I go

haram pyramids
Cala Tool straight on
dilwa'ti now
baCdeen later, then
baCd bukra the day after tomorrow
litneen Monday
Tayyaara (pl Tayyaaraat) aeroplane
SubH morning
Duhr noon
baCd iDDuhr afternoon
tazkara (pl tazaakir) ticket
dáraga class
taman price
raSiif platform
'aTr train

Explanations

● To ask 'where is ...?':
il'utiil **feen?** or
feen il'utiil?

● **Near or far**

'urayyib (min)	near (to)
biℓiid (min)	far (from)

da 'urayyib min hina? is that near here?
da biℓiid min il'utiil? is that far from the hotel?

● **Nearer and nearest**

The key word is **'a'rab.**
'a'rab 'agzakhaana - the nearest chemist (adjective first), *but*
fiih 'agzakhaana 'a'rab min il'utiil? - is there a chemist nearer to the hotel? (adjective second).

● **First and second**

	m	*f*
1st	'awwil	'uula
2nd	taani	tanya

You'll hear the masculine versions when you're being told which street to take:

'awwil		ℓala lyimiin	1st on the right
taani	**shaariℓ**	ℓala shshimaal	2nd on the left

and the feminine versions when you're asked if you want to travel 1st or 2nd class (notice that here they follow the noun):
dáraga 'uula walla dáraga tanya?

● The 'I' and 'you' forms of 'go' and 'take' are:

aakhud	I take	aruuh	I go
taakhud	you *(m)* take	tiruuH	you *(m)* go
takhdi	you *(f)* take	tiruuHi	you *(f)* go

Any of these forms can follow **mumkin:**
mumkin aakhud waHda? can I take one?
'aywa, mumkin taakhud waHda yes, you can take one

The imperatives of these are:
khud! *(to a man)*
khudi! *(to a woman)* take!

ruuH! *(to a man)*
ruuHi! *(to a woman)*   go!

The other verb 'go' which you'll hear in street directions (meaning 'go on') is:

amshi   I go
timshi   you *(m and f)* go
imshi!   go! *(m and f)*
imshi ʕala Tool!   go straight on!

● To say 'must':

use **laazim** (it is necessary), which is invariable and works like **mumkin** (see p38):

laazim taakhud taksi   you must take a taxi
laazim tiruuH il'utiil   you must go to the hotel

● **ʕaawiz** and **ʕawza** ('want') also work like **mumkin**, except that there are separate masculine and feminine forms:

I want to ...
ʕaawiz | aʕmil tilifoon
ʕawza | aruuH 'aSwaan

You want to .../do you want to ...?
ʕaawiz tishrab 'ahwa? *(to a man)*
ʕawza tiruuHi ilharam? *(to a woman)*

● More times and dates

To talk about fractions of the hour, say **nuSS** (half), **rubʕ** (quarter) and **tilt** (third, ie twenty minutes):

issaaʕa talaata w nuSS   it's (*or* at) half past three
issaaʕa tamanya w rubʕ   it's (*or* at) quarter past eight
issaaʕa itneen wi tilt   it's (*or* at) two twenty

If minutes are referred to, the ordinary numbers are used:

issaaʕa waHda w ʕáshara   ten past one

To say 'a quarter to ...' or 'ten to ...', use illa (less):

issaaƐa arbaƐa illa rubƐ   a quarter to four
issaaƐa talaata illa Ɛáshara/khamsa   ten/five to three

Days of the week are given on p74-75, together with the months.

yoom litneen (*lit* 'day two' of the Muslim week) is Monday. Often yoom is omitted: litneen.

Days of the month are simple: the appropriate number is used before the name of the month:

khamastaashar fibraayir (on) the 15th February
sitta mayyu   (on) the 6th May

● In chapter 3, a girl said mumkin ashuufha? (can I see it?), talking about the camera.
In this chapter, at the station the ticket clerk says tamanha khamsa gineeh (*lit* its cost is £5). The feminine -ha shows he's talking about tazkara (ticket) - another feminine noun.

Additional vocabulary

muwaSalaat *transport*	asaafir *I travel, leave*
maHaTTa *station, stop*	badri *early*
maHaTTit il'aTr *railway station*	wakhri *late*
	maftuuH *open*
'utubiis (*pl* 'utubisaat) *bus*	ma'fuul *closed*
maHaTTit il'utubiis *bus stop*	maktab ilbariid *post office*
Ɛarabiyya *car*	maktab SiyaaHa *tourist office*
⌐sayyaara, *pl* sayyaraat *car*⌐	
b il'aTr *by train*	'ism buliis *police station*
b il'utubiis *by bus*	mustashfa *hospital*
b ilƐarabiyya *by car*	sifaara *embassy*
sawwaa' *driver*	suu' *market, bazaar*
maTaar *airport*	

Worth knowing

Most towns and cities in the Middle East have a 'bazaar' area, part of which may specialise in tourist souvenirs, but where you will also find whole streets devoted to textiles, carpets, gold, jewellery, household goods, herbs and spices, and so on. Like Khan El Khalili in Cairo and the Hamidiyya bazaar in Damascus, they are often at the heart of the old city, by the walls of the earliest mosques and palaces. In North Africa the old part part of the city, the 'medina', is usually a maze of narrow lanes, surrounded by the original medieval walls.

Preferred modes of transport vary from country to country. The system of sharing taxis, especially between towns, is common; they generally operate between fixed points and you change to a 'local' taxi on your arrival. It's best to agree beforehand

on taxi fares, and to make it clear in advance if, for example, you want the driver to wait for you and then bring you back, with the words **mumkin tistanna hinaak, min faDlak?** (can you wait there, please?).

There is not a tradition of hitchhiking in the Middle East, and some countries actively discourage it. In any case, buses are extremely cheap and a very good way of meeting people.

The Egyptian Museum (**ilmatHaf ilmaSri**) in Cairo houses the world's most important collection of Egyptian antiquities dating back to the earliest civilisations. The collection includes monuments of the pharaohs, statues and jewellery, the treasure from the tomb of Tutankhamun and one of the great artistic masterpieces of all time - the gold mask of Tutankhamun.

Exercises

1 Tell someone 'I want ...':
a to take a taxi
b to go to the pyramids

c   to go to the hotel
d   to go to the museum
e   a ticket to Aswan

2   Tell a man 'You must ...':
a   take a taxi
b   see the pyramids
c   pay the bill
d   go to the chemist's

3   Now say the same things to a woman.

4   Tell the taxi driver to:
a   go straight on
b   turn left
c   take the first street on the right

5   You want to buy a first class return train
ticket to Aswan. Fill in your part of the
conversation.

Clerk	ayy*i* khidma? ɛaawiz tiruuH feen?
You	...
Clerk	dáraga 'uula walla dáraga tanya?
You	...
Clerk	raayiH walla raayiH gayy?
You	...
Clerk	tazkara dáraga 'uula tamanha sitta gineeh.
You	...
Clerk	shukran.

6   What times are being given here?
a   issaaɛa khamsa w nuSS
b   issaaɛa itneen wi rubɛ
c   issaaɛa ɛáshara w tilt
d   issaaɛa talaata illa khamsa
e   issaaɛa waHda illa rubɛ

6 Business and pleasure

Key expressions

ilmudiir mawguud?	is the manager in?
mish kida?	isn't it?/isn't that so?
batkallim Ɛárabi	I speak Arabic
a'addimlak	let me introduce you to
furSa saƐiida	pleased to meet you (*lit* a happy occasion)
Ɛandi maƐaad (maƐa)	I have an appointment (with)
kallimni	ring me
sharraftuuna	you have honoured us
nawwartu beetna	you have honoured us
mumkin awaSSalku?	can I give you *(pl)* a lift?
maƐa 'alf salaama	goodbye (*lit* with a thousand farewells)

Conversations

1 Making an appointment by phone.

Secretary	'alo?
kaamil	'alo? min faDlak, ilmudiir mawguud?
Secretary	'aywa, mawguud. issayyid kaamil, mish kida? di'ii'a waHda *(she puts him through).*
Director	'aywa ya sayyid kaamil. ayyi khidma?
kaamil	mumkin ashuufak baƐd bukra?
Director	Ɛandi maƐaad iSSubH. mumkin ashuufak issaaƐa talaata.
kaamil	Tayyib. in sha'allaah. 'alfi shukr.

2 zeenab asked people in a hotel which languages they spoke. First, two girls ...

zeenab	inti bititkallimi lughaat 'eeh, min faDlik?
Girl	ana batkallim Ɛárabi w ingiliizi shuwayya.
Girl	ana batkallim Ɛárabi, batkallim ingiliizi shuwayya, mish kitiir.
zeenab	bititkallimi faransaawi?
Girl	la'.
zeenab	bititkallimi almaani?
Girl	la'.
zeenab	Ɛárabi bass?
Girl	Ɛárabi w ingiliizi shuwayya.

... then a man

zeenab	inta bititkallim lughaat 'eeh?
Man	ana batkallim Ɛárabi w ingiliizi.
zeenab	bititkallim ingiliizi kwayyis walla nuSS nuSS walla shuwayya?
Man	shuwayya shuwayya!

3 Being introduced to someone at a party.

kaamil	misaa' ilkheer.
Hostess	misaa' innuur ... ahlan wa sahlan ... itfaDDalu ... sharraftuuna.
kaamil	shukran.
Hostess	ya duktuur saami, a'addimlak ilmuhandis kaamil Hasan, zimiili f ishshirka.
Dr saami	ahlan wa sahlan ... furSa saƐiida. itsharrafna.

4 Being offered a drink.

Hostess	tishrabu 'eeh ya gamaaƐa? fiih kulli Haaga.
leela	ashrab ƐaSiir lamuun min faDlik.
Hostess	w inta ya kaamil?
kaamil	ashrab biira min faDlik.

5 Are you happy in Cairo?

Host	inta mabSuuT fi maSr?
kaamil	'aywa, mabSuuT 'awi, innaas luTaaf giddan.
Host	w inti ya madaam?
leela	mabSuuTa 'awi, ilHamdu lillaah. bass ilgaww Harr shuwayya, mish kida?

6 Telling someone your plans.

kaamil	ɛandi maɛaad maɛa maHmuud makkaawi bukra. tiɛrafu?
Host	'aywa, raagil laTiif giddan. ilmaɛaad issaaɛa kam?
kaamil	issaaɛa khamsa w nuSS.
Host	inta w huwwa bass?
kaamil	la', ana w issayyid aHmad khaalid. raagil 'aɛmaal kuweeti.

7 Dinner is served!

Hostess	ɛaSiir taani, ya madaam?
leela	la', shukran, kifaaya kida.
Hostess	haniyyan ... il'akl gaahiz, ya gamaaɛa! itfaDDalu.

8 Asking someone to ring you.

kaamil	min faDlak, ya duktuur, kallimni yoom ilkhamiis iSSubH. nimrit tilifooni f ilbeet khamsa sabɛa talaata waaHid Sifr itneen. wi tilifoon ilmaktab, arbaɛa sitta tamanya khamsa waaHid waaHid.
Dr saami	Tayyib, in sha'allaah.

9 And farewells.

kaamil	Hafla mumtaaza, ya madaam. tislam ideeki. tiSbaHu ɛala kheer.
Hostess	tiSbaHu ɛala kheer.

Dr saami	Ɛandi sayyaara. mumkin awaSSalku?
kaamil	la', <u>sh</u>ukran. ilhutiil 'urayyib min hina.
Hostess	maƐa ssalaama! maƐa 'alf*i* salaama!

Vocabulary

mawguud *in, present*	aƐraf *I know*
sayyid *Mr*	raagil (*pl* riggaala) *man*
maƐaad *appointment*	raagil 'aƐmaal
'alf *a thousand*	*businessman*
bititkallim(i) *you speak*	kuweeti *Kuwaiti*
batkallim *I speak*	taani *another*
Ɛárabi *Arabic*	kifaaya *enough*
ingiliizi *English*	kida *like that, so*
faransaawi *French*	haniyyan *with enjoyment*
almaani *German*	gaahiz *ready*
nuSS nuSS *so so*	'akl *food*
zimiil (*pl* zamaayil)	il<u>kh</u>amiis *Thursday*
colleague	nimrit tilifoon *telephone*
<u>sh</u>irka (*pl* <u>sh</u>arikaat)	*number*
company	beet (*pl* buyuut) *house,*
ya gamaaƐa! *everybody*	*home*
kull*i* Haaga *everything*	f ilbeet *at home*
mabSuuT *pleased, happy*	Sifr *zero*
naas *people*	maktab *office*
laTiif (*pl* luTaaf)	Hafla *party, reception*
pleasant, kind	mumtaaz *lovely, splendid*
giddan *very*	tislam ideeki *bless your*
gaww *weather*	*hands*
Harr *hot*	sayyaara (*pl* sayyaraat) *car*
maƐa *with*	awaSSal *I give a lift*

Explanations

● To make an appointment with ...:
   mumkin aƐmil maƐaad maƐa ...?
   to which you add the time, day, etc.

● To ask 'Do you know him?': **tiƐrafu?**
   and 'Do you know her?': **tiƐrafha?**

- **b-** or **bi-** is used before verbs if the action is ongoing or habitual
  ana batkallim ʕárabi
  bashrab biira   I drink (*or* am drinking) beer

- **a'addim** means 'I introduce'.
  With **-lak** *(m)* or **-lik** *(f)*, it means 'I introduce to you ...'
  a'addimlak kaamil Hasan   let me introduce kaamil Hasan to you *(talking to a man)*

- The imperative of **akallim** (I talk to) is **kallim**. **-ni** (me) can be added to it:
  kallimni   talk to me/call me

- More plurals
  Adjectives, like nouns, have plural forms, but they are only used when referring to human beings.
  luTaaf is the plural of **laTiif** (nice):
  innaas luTaaf   the people are nice
  NB Plural nouns *not* referring to human beings take the *feminine singular* adjective:
  issandwitshaat kwayyisa the sandwiches are nice
  shikaat siyaHiyya travellers cheques

- **itfaDDalu** is the plural form of **itfaDDal** or **ıtfaDDali**; you might hear it when somebody is inviting everyone to come and eat.

- **tiSbaHu ʕala kheer** (good night) is the plural of **tiSbaH(i) ʕala kheer.**

- The commonest way of referring to a man politely is to use **issayyid** (Mr) followed by both his first and second names: **issayyid John Bates.** The equivalent term for a woman is **madaam**, and for a girl, **'anisa.**

idduktuur and **idduktuura** (Dr) are used before someone's first or second name.

il'ustaaz and **il'ustaaza** (*lit* Professor) are often used as a polite title for anyone with literary or academic qualifications.

Other job titles like **ilmuhandis** (engineer) are also used to introduce someone.

When addressing people, any of the following might be appropriate.

ya | **duktuur(a)**
   | **'ustaaz(a)**
   | **sayyid kamaal**
   | **madaam**

Worth knowing

Social visits in Arab countries can involve a wealth of polite exchanges of welcome and appreciation, some of which have cropped up in previous chapters.

If you are invited home, you might well hear **sharraftuuna** (*lit* you have honoured us), which can be said at the beginning or the end of a visit.

When being introduced, a common expression is **furSa saℰiida** (pleased to meet you, *lit* a happy occasion), and also **itsharraft** (I am honoured) and **itsharrafna** (we are honoured).

In business dealings, a common way of wishing someone 'good luck' is **b ittawfiiq** (*lit* with success), not forgetting the usual **in sha'allaah**.

To thank someone and say you've had enough, say: **shukran, kifaaya kida**. The reply will often be: **haniyyan** (glad you enjoyed it, *lit* with enjoyment), which is used after either food or drink.

To compliment the hostess on her hospitality:
tislam iddeeki (*lit* bless your hands)

As you leave someone's home, you will often hear
nawwartu beetna (you have brought light to our
house) and **maɛa 'alfi salaama** (with a thousand
goodbyes).

Additional vocabulary

miraati	*my wife*	walad (*pl* 'awlaad)	*son, child*
miraatak	*your wife*	SaaHib (*pl* 'aSHaab)	
goozi	*my husband*		*friend (m)*
goozik	*your husband*	SaHba	*friend* (f)

Exercises

1   You're making a phone call. Ask if the
following people are in:
a   the director
b   Dr White
c   Mr kamaal gindi
d   Mrs zeenab

2   Which of the following expressions would you
use A as a host or hostess, B as a guest?

a   sharraftuuna   A or B?
b   tislam 'ideeki   A or B?
c   'alfi shukr   A or B?
d   maɛa 'alfi salaama   A or B?
e   nawwartu beetna   A or B?

3   Read the following dialogue aloud twice then
answer the questions that follow.

Hostess	misaa' ilkheer ya duktuur ashraf.
	ahlan wa sahlan. nawwarti beetna.
Guest	ahlan biiki. izzayyik?
Hostess	kwayyisa, ilHamdu lillaah ...
	itfaDDal ... tishrab 'eeh?

Guest	mayya maᶜdaniyya bass, min faDlik.
Hostess	itfaDDal. tiᶜraf issaayyid <u>kh</u>aalid gamaal, raagil 'aᶜmaal min ba<u>gh</u>daad?
Guest	furSa saᶜiida. it<u>sh</u>arraft.

a   What time of day is it?
b   Who has just arrived?
c   What does he have to drink?
d   Who is he introduced to?
e   Where does the latter come from, and what's his job?

4   Ask a business acquaintance if you can see him …:
a   tomorrow
b   tomorrow afternoon
c   at half past four
d   on Monday
e   on Thursday morning
f   the day after tomorrow
g   in the hotel
h   at home

Abu Simbel

Can you 'GET BY'?

When you have finished the course, try your hand at this test. There is a possible maximum score of 65 points. Check your answers on p80. You might like to keep a record of your score, try the test again after a few days and see if you have improved.

First contacts

1 Say 'good evening'.
2 Reply to SabaaH il<u>kh</u>eer.
3 Reply to ahlan wa sahlan.
4 Ask a woman how she is.
5 Ask a man when you'll see him.
6 Ask a woman where she's from.
7 Say you're from England.
8 Say you're not from here.
9 Say you're a student (female).
10 Say thank you very much.
11 Say goodnight (to a couple).

Eating and drinking

Ask for the following:
12 two coffees and a tea
13 the menu, please (to the waiter)
14 three orange juices
15 one chicken and two grilled fish
16 a cheese sandwich
17 a vegetable soup
18 the bill, please (to a waitress)

Now ask:
19 what sandwiches there are.
20 what juices he's got.
21 if there's any wine here.
22 where the restaurant is.
23 what time breakfast is.

Shopping

Ask the price of:

24 that galabiyya ...
25 ... and that red one
26 the large bag
27 a kilo of potatoes
28 four stamps for England

Say:

29 That bag is very expensive.
30 Can I see a bigger size?
31 I want to buy a film for this camera.
32 Have you got a map of Cairo? (to a man)
33 Impossible. That's very expensive (referring to a souvenir camel).

Out and about

Ask for:

34 A ticket to Aswan ...
35 ... second class ...
36 ... return.

Say:

37 I want to go to the pyramids (you're a man).
38 I want to go the day after tomorrow (you're a woman).
39 Is the museum near here?
40 Where's the nearest telephone?
41 Is there a plane in the afternoon?
42 Can I take a taxi?
43 Straight on here and second street on the left.
44 Is this the train for Port Said?

In a hotel

45 Ask the receptionist if he has a room with bath.
46 Say you haven't got a reservation.
47 Ask if you can make a phone call from here.
48 Say you want to change some sterling.
49 Say 'room number 213'.

50 Ask where the lavatory is.
51 Say you have travellers cheques.
52 Say the phone isn't working.
53 Say 'that's for you' (when tipping a man).

Social encounters

Ask:
54 What would you like to drink? (to a man)
55 Do you speak English? (to a woman)
56 Do you know Dr saami? (to a man)
57 Are you happy in London? (to a woman)
58 Another juice?

Say:
59 I have an appointment with Mr Hasan ...
60 ... at half past three.
61 Cairo is very big, isn't it?
62 What languages do you speak? (to a woman)
63 You speak a little Arabic ...
64 ... and French so so.

65 Finally, wish someone success.

Reference section

Language notes

● Nouns and adjectives
il- is prefixed to definite nouns and adjectives:

'akl kwayyis	nice food
il'akl ilkwayyis	the nice food

● A final **-a** indicates the feminine:

mudarris laTiif	a nice teacher *(m)*
mudarrisa laTiifa	a nice teacher *(f)*

● Demonstratives (this/that/these/those)
da *(m)*, **di** *(f)* and **dool** *(pl)* are added to definite nouns:

il'akl da	this/that food
ilmudiira di	this/that manageress
innaas dool	these/those people

da, **di** and **dool** can be used by themselves when referring to masculine, feminine or plural nouns:

da kwayyis	that *(m)* is fine
di kibiira	that *(f)* one is big
dool min landan	those are from London

● Plurals
-aat is often added to the singular:
dolaar - dolaraat   sandwit<u>sh</u> - sandwit<u>sh</u>aat
More usually the word changes internally, following one of half a dozen different 'patterns'. You just have to learn which plural pattern each noun takes.
The commonest patterns:

kart	kuruut	'ir<u>sh</u>	'uruu<u>sh</u>
<u>sh</u>anTa	<u>sh</u>unaT	furSa	furaS

maktab	makaatib	tazkara	tazaakir
maTℰam	maTaa9im	sigaara	sagaayir
isbuuℰ	asabiiℰ	miftaaH	mafatiiH
SaaHib	'aSHaab	Sanf	'aSnaaf
walad	'awlaad	nooℰ	'anwaaℰ

After a plural noun a *feminine singular* adjective is usually used:

sandwitshaat kibiira   big sandwiches

but the plural form of the adjective is used if the noun refers to human beings:

naas luTaaf   nice people

This is a common pattern for plural adjectives:

Sughayyar   Sughaar

● The dual

Instead of using the number 'two', the noun takes the 'dual' ending **-een**:

yoom day   **yomeen** two days

In feminine nouns the **-a** ending changes to **-teen**:

Haaga thing   **Hagteen** two things

When ordering food or drink, the singular noun is used with all numbers:

itneen biira   two beers

arbaℰa shaay   four teas

● Comparatives and superlatives

The same basic pattern is used to make both the comparative (eg bigger) and superlative (eg biggest)

kibiir big   **'akbar** bigger, biggest

rikhiiS cheap   **'arkhaS** cheaper, cheapest

When it means 'bigger', 'cheaper' etc, it *follows* the noun:

Haaga 'arkhaS   something cheaper

and it comes *before* the noun when it means 'biggest', 'cheapest', etc:

'arkhaS Haaga   the cheapest thing

- **Pronouns**

As the subject of a sentence they take the following forms:

ana	I	iHna	we
inta	you *(m)*		
inti	you *(f)*	intu	you *(pl)*
huwwa	he		
hiyya	she	humma	they

Following a noun or preposition they take the forms:

-i	beeti	my home
-ak	beetak	your *(m)* home
-ik	beetik	your *(f)* home
-u	beetu	his home
-ha	beetha	her home
-na	beetna	our home
-ku	beetku	your *(pl)* home
-hum	beethum	their home

After a preposition:

'uddaami	in front of me
Candu	*lit* with him, *ie* he has

After verbs, almost the same forms are used; only the 'me' form is different:

kallim speak to **kallimni** speak to me

- A regular verb in the present tense:

ashrab	I drink	nishrab	we drink
tishrab	you *(m)* drink	tishrabu	you *(pl)*
tishrabi	you *(f)* drink		drink
yishrab	he drinks	yishrabu	they drink
tishrab	she drinks		

ie various prefixes and suffixes are added to the base -**shrab**-.

These forms can follow **mumkin** (can), **laazim** (must) and **Caawiz** or **Cawza** (want):

mumkin ashrab?	can I drink?
laazim tishrab	you *(m)* must drink
Caawiz yishrab	he wants to drink

- **bi-** precedes the verb if the action is habitual or ongoing:
  hiyya bitishrab mayya she (usually) drinks (*or* is now drinking) water
  bititkallim ingiliizi? do you speak English?

- Imperatives
  The initial **t-** of the second person is lost:
  ishrab!   drink! *(m)*
  ishrabi!   drink! *(f)*
  ishrabu!   drink! *(pl)*

  For verbs like **ashuuf** (see) and **aruuH** (go), where the base begins with a single consonant, the initial **-i** is lost as well:
  shuuf!   look! *(m)*
  shuufi!   look! *(f)*
  shuufu!   look! *(pl)*

- Negatives
  In 'verbless' sentences like
  ana min landan   I (am) from London
  huwwa laTiif   he (is) kind, pleasant
  mish is inserted:
  ana mish min landan
  huwwa mish laTiif etc

  With verbs, **ma-** and **-sh** are placed before and after the verb:
  mayishuufsh   he doesn't see
  The same is true for **fiih** and **ɛand-**:

mafiish 'akl	there is no food
maɛandiish sayyaara	I don't have a car
maɛandaksh sandwitshaat?	don't you have sandwiches?

- Days of the week
  yoom litneen   Monday
  yoom ittalaat   Tuesday

yoom larba{ Wednesday
yoom ilkhamiis Thursday
yoom ilgum{a Friday
yoom issabt Saturday
yoom ilHadd Sunday
yoom (day) can be omitted.

● Months of the year

yanaayir	January	**yulyu**	July
fibraayir	February	**aghusTus**	August
maaris	March	**sibtimbir**	September
abriil	April	**uktuubar**	October
mayyu	May	**nuvimbir**	November
yunyu	June	**disimbir**	December

● The seasons

irrabii{	the spring	**iSSeef**	the summer
ilkhariif	the autumn	**ishshita**	the winter

● Numbers

0	**Sifr**	14	**arba{taashar**
1	**waaHid**	15	**khamastaashar**
2	**itneen**	16	**sittaashar**
3	**talaata**	17	**sab{ataashar**
4	**arba{a**	18	**tamantaashar**
5	**khamsa**	19	**tisa{taashar**
6	**sitta**	20	**{ishriin**
7	**sab{a**	30	**talatiin**
8	**tamanya**	40	**arbi{iin**
9	**tis{a**	50	**khamsiin**
10	**{ashara**	60	**sittiin**
11	**Hidaashar**	70	**sab{iin**
12	**itnaashar**	80	**tamaniin**
13	**talattaashar**	90	**tis{iin**

Any number over 10 is followed by a *singular* noun:

Hidaashar yoom	11 days
talatiin Taalib	30 students

To make numbers like twenty-five, fifty-three,

say 'five and twenty', 'three and fifty':

25 <u>kh</u>amsa w Ɛi<u>sh</u>riin
53 talaata w <u>kh</u>amsiin

100	miyya	1000	'alf
200	miteen	2000	'alfeen
300	tultumiyya	3000	talat alaaf
400	rubɛumiyya	4000	arbaɛt alaaf
500	<u>kh</u>umsumiyya	5000	<u>kh</u>amast alaaf
600	suttumiyya	6000	sitt alaaf
700	subɛumiyya	7000	sabaɛt alaaf
800	tumnumiyya	8000	tamant alaaf
900	tusɛumiyya	9000	tisaɛt alaaf

When 100 - 900 are followed by a noun,
-**miyya** becomes -**miit**:

£400   rubɛumiit gineeh
300,000   tultumiit 'alf
400,000   rubɛumiit 'alf

Key to exercises

Chapter 1

1   a   ana min ingiltira.
    b   ismi John.

2   a   ana min maSr. (or ana min ilqaahira).
    b   ismi Taari'.

3   a   afternoon or evening.
    b   morning
    c   any time of day

4   a   misaa' innuur.
    b   SabaaH innuur.
    c   ahlan biik(i).

5   a   ahlan wa sahlan. ismak 'eeh?
    b   inta mineen?

6   a   ahlan wa sahlan. ismik 'eeh?
    b   inti mineen?

7   a   SabaaH il<u>kh</u>eer ya mu'nis.
    b   (inta) izzayyak?
    c   a<u>sh</u>uufak imta?
    d   in <u>sh</u>a'allaah.

Chapter 2

1 a   ʿaSiir burTuʿaan min faDlak.
   b   itneen biira min faDlak.
   c   sandwitsh min faDlak.
   d   'ahwa maZbuuT min faDlak.
   e   shurbit khuDaar min faDlak.
   f   ilHisaab min faDlak.

2 min faDlak would become min faDlik.

3 a   fiih 'ahwa?
   b   fiih ʿaSiir manga?
   c   fiih shurbit baSal?
   d   fiih ruzz?
   e   fiih sandwitshaat?

4 a   ʿandak 'ahwa?
   b   ʿandak ʿaSiir manga?
   c   ʿandak shurbit baSal?
   d   ʿandak ruzz?
   e   ʿandak sandwitshaat?

5 a   ʿandak sandwitshaat gibna?
   b   fiih nibiit hina?
   c   ʿandak mayya maʿdaniyya?
   d   ilHisaab min faDlak.
   e   shukran.

Chapter 3

1 a   a big bag
   b   the big bag
   c   the bag is big
   d   this bag is big

2 a   ʿandak kuruut buSTaal min faDlak?
   b   ʿandak Tawaabiʿ min faDlak?
   c   ʿandak film mulawwan min faDlak?
   d   ʿandak shanTa kibiira min faDlak?
   e   ʿandak gallabiyya Hamra?

3 a   mumkin ashuuf gallabiyya?
   b   mumkin ashuuf ilkamera di?
   c   mumkin ashuuf ma'aas 'akbar?
   d   mumkin ashuuf Sanf 'arkhaS?

4 a   bi kam kiilu ilburTuʿaan?
   b   bi kam nuSS kiilu illamuun?
   c   bi kam itneen kiilu ilmooz?
   d   bi kam nuSS kiilu issukkar?

5 a   di ghalya 'awi
   b   da ghaali 'awi
   c   da ghaali 'awi
   d   di ghalya 'awi

6 a fiih <u>sh</u>anTa 'akbar?
    b fiih fustaan 'a<u>Sgh</u>ar?
    c fiih kamera 'ar<u>kh</u>aS?
    d fiih Sanf 'aHsan?

Chapter 4

1 a fiih Hammaam?
    b fiih du<u>shsh</u>?
    c fiih tilifoón?
    d fiih mayya su<u>kh</u>na?

2 a ilHammaam ɛaTlaan.
    b iddu<u>shsh</u> ɛaTlaan.
    c ittilifoon ɛaTlaan.
    d mafii<u>sh</u> mayya su<u>kh</u>na.

3 a mumkin adfaɛ ilHisaab?
    b mumkin aɛmil tilifoon?
    c mumkin a<u>gh</u>ayyar dolaraat?

4 SabaaH innuur.
    fiih 'ooDa faDya?
    bi siriir waaHid.
    lelteen.
    bi kam il'ooDa?

Chapter 5

1 ɛaawiz ... (or ɛawza ...)
    a aa<u>kh</u>ud taksi.
    b aruuH ilharam.
    c aruuH il'utiil.
    d aruuH ilmatHaf.
    e tazkara li 'aSwaan.

2 laazim ...
    a taa<u>kh</u>ud taksi.
    b ti<u>sh</u>uuf ilharam.
    c tidfaɛ ilHisaab.
    d tiruuH il'agza<u>kh</u>aana.

3 laazim
    a ta<u>kh</u>di taksi
    b ti<u>sh</u>uufi ilharam.
    c tidfaɛi ilHisaab.
    d tiruuHi il'agza<u>kh</u>aana

4 a (im<u>sh</u>i) ɛala Tool.
    b (im<u>sh</u>i) ɛala <u>shsh</u>imaal.
    c (taa<u>kh</u>uud) 'awwil <u>sh</u>aariɛ ɛala lyimiin.

5 (ana) ɛaawiz aruuH 'aSwaan.
dáraga 'uula.
raayiH gayy.
itfaDDal.

6 a 5.30 b 2.15 c 10.20 d 2.55 e 12.45

Chapter 6

1 a ilmudiir mawguud?
b idduktuur White mawguud?
c issayyid kamaal gindi mawguud?
d madaam zeenab mawguuda?

2 a A b B c B d A or B e A

3 a afternoon or evening
b Dr ashraf
c mineral water
d Mr khaalid gamaal
e He's a businessman from Baghdad.

4 mumkin ashuufak ...
a bukra?
b bukra baɛd iDDuhr?
c issaaɛa arbaɛa w nuSS?
d (yoom) litneen?
e (yoom) ilkhamiis iSSubH?
f baɛd bukra?
g f il'utiil?
h f ilbeet?

Answers to 'Can you get by?'

1. misaa' il<u>kh</u>eer.
2. SabaaH innuur.
3. ahlan biik (to a man); ahlan biiki (to a woman)
4. izzayyik?
5. a<u>sh</u>uufak imta?
6. inti mineen?
7. ana min ingiltira.
8. ana mi<u>sh</u> min hina.
9. ana Taaliba.
10. 'alf <u>sh</u>ukr.
11. tiSbaHu Ɛala <u>kh</u>eer.
12. itneen 'ahwa w waaHid <u>sh</u>aay.
13. ilminyu, min faDlak.
14. talaata Ɛa Siir burTu'aan.
15. waaHid firaa<u>kh</u> w itneen samak ma<u>sh</u>wi.
16. (waaHid) sandwit<u>sh</u> gibna.
17. (waaHid) <u>sh</u>urbit <u>kh</u>uDaar.
18. ilHisaab, min faDlik.
19. fiih sandwit<u>sh</u>aat 'eeh?
20. Ɛandak Ɛa Siir 'eeh?
21. fiih nibiit hina?
22. ilmaTƐam feen?
23. ilfiTaar issaaƐa kam?
24. bi kam ilgallabiyya di ...?
25. ... w ilHamra di?
26. bi kam i<u>shsh</u>anTa ilkibiira?
27. bi kam kiilu ilbaTaaTis?
28. bi kam arbaƐ Tawaabiʕ l ingiltira?
29. i<u>shsh</u>anTa di <u>gh</u>alya 'awi.
30. mumkin a<u>sh</u>uuf ma'aas 'akbar?
31. Ɛaawiz (or Ɛawza) film l ilkámera di?
32. Ɛandak <u>kh</u>ariiTa l ilqaahira?
33. mi<u>sh</u> mumkin. da <u>gh</u>aali 'awi.
34. tazkara li 'aSwaan
35. ...dáraga tanya
36. ...raayiH gayy.
37. Ɛaawiz aruuH ilharam.
38. Ɛawza aruuH baƐd bukra.
39. ilmatHaf 'urayyib min hina?
40. feen 'a'rab tilifoon?
41. fiih Tayyaara iDDuhr?
42. mumkin aa<u>kh</u>ud taksi?
43. Ɛala Tool hina wi taani <u>sh</u>aariƐ Ɛala <u>sh</u>shimaal.
44. da 'aTr buur saƐiid?
45. Ɛandak 'ooDa bi Hammaam?
46. maƐandii<u>sh</u> Hagz.
47. mumkin aƐmil tilifoon min hina?

48 ana ʕaawiz (*or* ʕawza) aghayyar istirliini.
49 'ooDa nimra miteen wi talataashar.
50 ittwalett feen?
51 ʕandi shikaat siyaHiyya.
52 ittilifoon ʕaTlaan (*or* mish shaghghaal).
53 da ʕalashaanak.
54 tishrab 'eeh?
55 (inti) bititkallimi ingiliizi?
56 (inta) tiʕraf idduktuur saami?
57 (inti) mabSuuTa fi landan?
58 ʕaSiir taani?
59 ʕandi maʕaad maʕa issayyid Hasan ...
60 ... issaaʕa talaata w nuSS.
61 ilqaahira kibiira 'awi, mish kida? (*or* maSr
      kibiira, mish kida?)
62 (inti) bititkallimi lughaat 'eeh?
63 (ana) batkallim ʕárabi shuwayya ...
64 ... wi faransaawi nuSS nuSS.
65 b ittawfiiq, in shaʔallaah.

Word list

The following is a list of the words appearing in the conversations in the six chapters.
The alphabetical order used is:
' a b d D E f g gh h H i k kh l m n o q r s S sh t T u v w y z Z ξ

In addition, related forms are shown thus wherever they seem valuable:

plurals	Suura (*pl* Suwar)
masculines	Hamra (*m* 'aHmar)
feminines	gaahiz (*f* gahza)

Verbs are given in the first person singular form, eg

ashtiri *I buy*
ashuuf *I see*

so if you are looking for the words tishrab or tiξraf, look under ashrab or aξraf. A fuller list of verb forms can be found on p73-74.

'a'rab *nearer, nearest*
'aasif (*f* 'asfa) *sorry*
'agzakhaana *chemist*
'ahwa *coffee*
'aHsan *better, best*
'akbar *bigger, biggest*
'akl *food*
'alf *a thousand*
'alf shukr *many thanks*
'alo *hallo (on phone)*
'arkhaS *cheaper; cheapest*
'asanSiir *lift*
'asfa *sorry (f)*
'aSwaan *Aswan*
'aTr *train*
'awi *very*
'awwil (*f* 'uula) *first*
'aywa *yes*
'eeh? *what?*
'irsh (*pl* 'uruush) *piastre*
'izaaza *bottle*
'ooDa (*pl* 'owaD) *room*
'uddaam *in front of*
'umaash *material*

'urayyib (min) *near (to)*
'uruush *piastres*
'utiil *hotel*
'uula *first (f)*

a

a'addimlak ... *let me introduce ... to you*
aakul *I eat*
aakhud *I take*
adfaξ *I pay*
aghayyar *I change*
ahlan *hallo, nice to meet you*
ahlan biik(i) *reply to ahlan or ahlan wa sahlan*
ahlan wa sahlan *hallo, nice to meet you, welcome*
akallim *I speak (to)*
aktib *I write*
almaani *German*
amDi *I sign*
amshi *I go*
ana *I*
arbaξa *four*
arbiξiin *forty*

aruuH I go (to)
ashrab I drink
ashtiri I buy
ashuuf I see
atkallim I speak
awaSSal I give a lift
ayyi khidma can I help you?;
    don't mention it
aɛmil tilifoon I make a
    phone call
aɛraf I know

b

balad town, country
bank bank
banyu bath
babuur passport
bass but; only
baSal onion
batkallim I speak
baTaaTis potatoes
baɛd after
baɛd bukra (the) day after
    tomorrow
baɛdeen later, then
baɛd iDDuhr afternoon
beeD eggs
beet (pl buyuut) house, home
bi with
bi balaash free, for nothing
bi kam? how much?
bi kheer fine, well
bi kull suruur with the
    greatest pleasure; certainly
biira beer
bisilla peas
biɛiid (min) far (from)
bukra tomorrow
burTu'aan orange
buur saɛiid Port Said

d

da this, that (m)
dáraga class
di this, that (f)
di'ii'a moment, minute
dilwa'ti now
dolaar (pl dolaraat) dollar
door floor
duktuur (f -a) doctor

dushsh shower

D

Duhr (after)noon

f

faaDi (f faDya) empty, free
falaafil chick peas or beans
faransaawi French
farawla strawberry
feen? where?
fi in, at
fiih there is/are
film (pl 'aflaam) film
firaakh chicken
fiTaar breakfast
furSa saɛiida pleased to
    meet you
fuul cooked beans

g

gaahiz (f gahza) ready
gallabiyya (pl -aat)
    galabiyya
gamaaɛa everyone
gamal camel
gambari prawns
gawaafa guava
gaww weather
gibna cheese
giddan very
gineeh pound
grepfruut grapefruit

gh

ghaali (f ghalya) expensive

h

haniyyan glad you enjoyed it
haram pyramids
hina here
hinaak there
hiyya she
hutiil hotel
huwwa he

H

HaaDir certainly, at once
Haaga (pl Hagaat) thing,
    something

Haaga kamaan? (*or* Haaga · tanya?) *anything else?*

Hafla (*pl* Hafalaat) *party, reception*

Hagz *reservation*

Hammaam *bathroom*

Hamra (*m* 'aHmar) *red*

Harr *hot*

Hilw *beautiful, fine, sweet*

Hisaab *bill*

i

iddiini *give me*

ilHamdu lillaah *fine (God be praised)*

ilkhamiis *Thursday*

ilkhartuum *Khartoum*

illa *less, without*

ilqaahira *Cairo*

ilＣafw *not at all; don't mention it*

imta? *when?*

ingiliizi *English*

ingiltira *England*

in sha'allaah *God willing; I hope so*

inta *you* (m)

inti *you* (f)

iskindriyya *Alexandria*

ism *name*

issaaＣa kam? *what time is it?; at what time?*

issudaan *Sudan*

issuＣudiyya *Saudi Arabia*

istirliini *sterling*

iSSumaal *Somalia*

itfaDDal(i) *here you are; help yourself*

itnaashar *twelve*

itneen *two*

izzayyak? *how are you* (to a man)

izzayyik? *how are you?* (to a woman)

k

kallimni *ring me*

kam? *how much?; how many?*

kamaan *also*

kámera *camera*

kart (*pl* kuruut) buSTaal *postcard*

kibiir *big*

kibda *liver*

kida *like that, so*

kifaaya *enough*

kitiir *a lot, much, many*

kufta *meat balls*

kull *each, every*

kuweeti *Kuwaiti*

kwayyis *fine, well*

kh

khamsa *five*

khan ilkhaliili *Khan El Khalili*

khariiTa *map*

khidma *service*

khuDaar *vegetables*

l

la' *no*

laazim *it is necessary, have to, must*

lamuun *lemon*

landan *London*

laTiif (*pl* luTaaf) *nice, pleasant*

leela (*pl* layaali) *night*

li *to, for*

litneen *Monday*

lugha (*pl* -aat) *language*

m

ma'aas *size*

mabSuuT *happy*

mafiish *there isn't/aren't*

maktab (*pl* makaatib) *office*

malyaan *full*

manga *mango*

maSr *Egypt, Cairo (see p19)*

mashwi *grilled*

matHaf *museum*

maTＣam (*pl* maTaaＣim) *restaurant*

mawguud *available, in*

mayya (maＣdaniyya) *(mineral) water*

maZbuuT *right; exact;*

medium sweet

maʕa *with*

maʕa ssalaama *goodbye*

maʕaad *appointment*

maʕandiish *I haven't*

midaan *square*

midaan ittaHriir *Liberation Square*

min *from*

mineen? *where from?*

min faDlak *please* (to a man)

min faDlik *please* (to a woman)

minyu *menu*

misaa' ilkheer *good afternoon/evening*

misaa' innuur *reply to misaa' ilkheer*

mish *not*

mish kida? *isn't it?; isn't that so?*

miteen *two hundred*

mitr *metre*

mudarris *(f -a) teacher*

mudiir *(f -a) manager, director*

muftaaH *key*

muhandis *(f -a) engineer*

mulawwan *coloured, in colour*

mumkin *it is possible*

mumtaaz *lovely, splendid*

n

naas *people*

nawwartu beetna *you have honoured us*

nibiit *wine*

nimra *number*

nimrit tilifoon *telephone number*

nuSS *half*

nuSS nuSS *so so*

nuuba *Nubia*

r

raagil *(pl riggaala) man*

raagil 'aʕmaal *businessman*

raayiH *single*

raayiH gayy *return*

raSiif *platform*

rikhiiS *cheap*

rubʕ *quarter*

ruzz *rice*

s

sa'ʕa *cold*

saaʕa *hour; time*

sabaanikh *spinach*

sabʕa *seven*

sabʕiin *seventy*

samak *fish*

sanduu' *box*

sandwitsh *(pl -aat) sandwich*

sayyaara *(pl sayyaraat) car*

sayyid *Mr*

siriir *bed*

sitta *six*

sittiin *sixty*

sukhna *hot*

suttumiyya *six hundred*

S

SabaaH ilkheer *good morning*

SabaaH innuur *reply to SabaaH ilkheer*

Sanf *(pl 'aSnaaf) kind, sort*

Sifr *zero*

SubH *morning*

Suura *(pl Suwar) picture*

sh

shaariʕ *(pl shawaariʕ) street*

shaay *tea*

shanTa *(pl shunaT) bag*

sharraftuuna *you have honoured us*

shiik *(pl shikaat) siyaHiyya travellers cheque*

shiisha *hubble bubble*

shimaal *left*

shirka *(pl sharikaat) company*

shukran *thank you*

shurba *soup*

shuwayya *a little, quite*

t

taani *(f tanya) second; other*

taksi *(pl taksiyyaat) taxi*

talaata *three*

talatiin *thirty*
taman *cost, price*
tamanya *eight*
tanya *second (f)*
tazkara (*pl* tazaakir) *ticket*
tiSbaH ⲥala kheer *good night*
tilifoon *telephone*
tilivizyoon *television*
tilt *a third; twenty minutes*
tislam ideeki *thank you for your hospitality (lit bless your hands)*

T
Taabiⲥ (*pl* Tawaabiⲥ) *stamp*
Taalib (*f* -a) *student*
Tabⲥan *of course*
Tayyaara (*pl* Tayyaraat) *aeroplane*
Tayyib *OK, well now ...*
Taⲥmiyya *fried cakes of ground beans*

w
waaHid (*f* waHda) *one*
walla *or*
wi *and*

y
ya *form of address (see p17)*
y afandim *sir*
ya beeh *sir*
ya madaam *madam*
yimiin *right*
yoom (*pl* 'ayyaam) *day*

z
zimiil (*pl* zamaayil) *colleague*

ⲥ
ⲥaawiz (*or* ⲥaayiz) *I/you/he want(s)*
ⲥafwan *not at all; don't mention it*
ⲥala *on*
ⲥala Tool *straight on*
ⲥalashaan *for*
ⲥandi *I have*
ⲥárabi *Arabic*
ⲥaSiir *juice*
ⲥaTlaan *not working*
ⲥawza (*or* ⲥayza) *I/you/she want(s)*
ⲥishriin *twenty*

An introduction to Arabic writing

The purpose of this section is to help you recognise public signs, posters, notices and the like which you will see on visits to Arab countries.

Arabic is written from right to left, and its alphabet has 29 letters. Most of these letters are easy to pronounce for English speakers, as equivalent sounds exist in English (see Pronunciation guide, p8). The Arabic alphabet and the corresponding transliterations are as follows:

NB 'th' is pronounced as in 'thanks' and '<u>th</u>' as in 'that'

<u>kh</u>	H	j or g	th	t	b	a	'glottal stop
خ	ح	ج	ث	ت	ب	أ	ء

D	S	<u>sh</u>	s	z	r	<u>th</u>	d
ض	ص	ش	س	ز	ر	ذ	د

k	q	f	<u>gh</u>	ع	Z	T
ك	ق	ف	غ	ع	ظ	ط

y	w	h	n	m	l
ي	و	هـ	ن	م	ل

These three letters are used as long vowels:
aa ا   ii ي or ـي   uu و

The glottal stop ء is usually 'carried' on top of one
of the long vowel symbols; eg أ = 'a

NB The sound represented by ذ (as in 'that') has
changed into 'd' or 'z' in spoken Egyptian Arabic,
and the sound represented by ث (as in 'thanks')
has changed into 't' or 's'.

There are vowel 'marks' which are not included in
the 29 letters of the alphabet. They *can* be shown,
written above or below the consonant (eg تَ = ta,
تِ = ti, تُ = tu), but in writing and print the
marks are nearly always omitted, (a bit like English
shorthand) as those who know the language well
can recognise the words without them.

If a consonant is doubled, a ّ appears above the
letter: (eg حمّام = Hammaam, ستّة = sitta).

Unlike English, Arabic letters are 'joined up' into
words not only in writing but in print as well. The
'joining' system, however, is subject to certain
rules to avoid risk of confusion and also for
aesthetic purposes (Arabs are very proud of the
beauty of the Arabic script).

1 The following letters never join the letter following them.

و   ز   ر   ذ   د   أ   ا

2 The following letters 'shrink' when they are joined up, ie they become narrower.

ق   ف   ن   ي   ث   ت   ب

3 The following letters lose their tails or 'flourishes' when they join. The letters are still easily recognisable after their tails are cut.

ل   غ   ع   ض   ص   ش   س   خ   ح   ج

4 The final letter in all words is written in full, that is to say, it retains its original shape as given in the alphabet list above.

5 The following table shows those letters that change depending on whether they come at the beginning, in the middle or at the end of a word.

End		Middle	Beginning
ة	ت	ـتـ	تـ
ع	ع	ـعـ	عـ
غ	غ	ـغـ	غـ
ك		ـكـ	كـ
ه	ه	ـهـ	هـ
ى	ي	ـيـ	يـ

NB ة is a feminine ending, so it is always a final letter. If joined to the previous letter, it is ـة. The final letter ى can stand for a final 'a'.

The following shows how separate letters join together to form words according to the above rules. We have used each letter in the three possible positions - beginning, middle and end. Translations are not given as the words are intended simply as examples of the appearance of the writing system. Remember, you are reading from right to left.

a	أ	أكل / أ ك ل	سأل / س أ ل	بدأ / ب د أ
b	ب	بيت / ب ي ت	سبت / س ب ت	كتب / ك ت ب
t	ت	تين / ت ي ن	كتب / ك ت ب	بنت / ب ن ت
t	ة	قهوة / ق هـ و ة	ة	حفلة
th	ث	ثلج / ث ل ج	نثر / ن ث ر	لبث / ل ب ث
j/g	ج	جمل / ج م ل	سجد / س ج د	نتج / ن ت ج
H	ح	حرب / ح ر ب	بحر / ب ح ر	لمح / ل م ح
kh	خ	خبز / خ ب ز	دخل / د خ ل	صرخ / ص ر خ
d	د	دخل / د خ ل	بدر / ب د ر	بلد / ب ل د
th	ذ	ذهب / ذ هـ ب	بذر / ب ذ ر	لذيذ / ل ذ ي ذ
r	ر	رجل / ر ج ل	برد / ب ر د	أجر / أ ج ر

z	ز	ز ي ت / زيت	ن ز ف / نزف	ب ر ز / برز
s	س	س ت ر / ستر	م س ك / مسك	ل م س / لمس
sh	ش	ش ك ر / شكر	ر ش د / رشد	ق ر ش / قرش
S	ص	ص ر ف / صرف	م ص ر / مصر	ح ر ص / حرص
D	ض	ض ي ف / ضيف	ن ض ر / نضر	ع ر ض / عرض
T	ط	ط ر ب / طرب	ق ط ر / قطر	ن ف ط / نفط
Z	ظ	ظ ب ي / ظبي	ن ظ ر / نظر	و ع ظ / وعظ
ع	ع	ع ل م / علم	س ع د / سعد	م ن ع ب ر ع / منع برع
gh	غ	غ ر ب / غرب	ب غ د ا د / بغداد	ب ل غ ف ر غ / بلغ فرغ
f	ف	ف ت ح / فتح	ل ف ت / لفت	أ ل ف / ألف
q	ق	ق ل ب / قلب	ن ق ل / نقل	ح ل ق / حلق

				k ك
س م ك	م ك ت ب	ك ت ب		
سمك	مكتب	كتب		
				l ل
ح م ل	ب ل د	ل ب س		
حمل	بلد	لبس		
				m م
ق ل م	س م ك	م ل ك		
قلم	سمك	ملك		
				n ن
ل ب ن	ب ن ت	ن ش ر		
لبن	بنت	نشر		
				h هـ
ر ف ه ب ل د ه	س هـ ل	هـ ر م		
رفه بلده	سهل	هرم		
				w و
ح ل و	ف و ل	و ل د		
حلو	فول	ولد		
				y ي
ل ق ي هـ د ى	ن يـ ل	ي ج د		
لقي هدى	نيل	يجد		

Here is a list of some of the words and phrases
you will be most likely to see on signs and notices.
They are given with (a) a 'spoken' form following
the transliteration system explained on pp8-10 and
(b) an English translation.

menu	ilminyu	المنيو
restaurant	maTɛam	مطعم
hotel	hutiil	هوتيل
hotel	funduq	فندق
WC	doorit mayya	دورة مياه

91

waaHid wi tisɛiin 91

gents	l irriggaal	للرجال
ladies	l issayyidaat	للسيّدات
danger	khaTar	خطر
exit	khuruug	خروج
no entry	mamnuuʕ iddukhuul	ممنوع الدخول
no smoking	mamnuuʕ ittadkhiin	ممنوع التدخين
no photographs	mamnuuʕ ittaSwiir	ممنوع التصوير
no parking	mamnuuʕ wuquuf issayyaraat	ممنوع وقوف السيّارات
bus stop	mawqaf il'utubiis	موقف الأوتوبيس
taxi rank	mawqaf ittaksi	موقف التاكسي
car park	mawqaf issayyaraat	موقف السيارات
post office	maktab ilbariid	مكتب البريد
information office	maktab ilistiʕlamaat	مكتب الاستعلامات
information	ilistiʕlamaat	الاستعلامات
tourist office	maktab issiyaaHa	مكتب السياحة
ticket window	shibbaak ittazaakir	شبّاك التذاكر
bank	maSraf	مصرف

bank	bank	بنك
bureau de change	maSraf taghyiir il۲umla	مصرف تغيير العملة
bureau de change	maktab Siraafa	مكتب صرافة
to the airport	ila lmaTaar	إلى المطار
to the station	ila lmaHaTTa	إلى المحطة
stop	qif	قف
customs	ilgamaarik	الجمارك
passports and visas	ilgawazaat w itta'shiiraat	الجوازات والتأشيرات
embassy	sifaara	سفارة
consulate	qunSuliyya	قنصلية
museum	matHaf	متحف
exhibition	ma۲raD	معرض
company	shirka	شركة
telephone	ittilifoon	التيليفون
telephone	ilhaatif	[الهاتف
telephones	tilifoonaat	تيليفونات
telegrams	tilighrafaat	تليغرافات
hospital	mustashfa	مستشفى
chemist's	'agzakhaana	أجزخانة
chemist's	Saydaliyya	صيدلية
police station	qism ilbuliis	قسم البوليس

| police station | markaz ishshurTa | مركز الشرطة] |
| cafe | maqha | مقهى |

In much of the Arab world, the following figures are used:

٩	٨	٧	٦	٥	٤	٣	٢	١	٠
9	8	7	6	5	4	3	2	1	0

Compound numbers are written from left to right as in English.

٧٨٦٤٣١٥	٣٥١٤٧٦ ت	١٩٨٥
7 8 6 4 3 1 5	Tel: 3 5 1 4 7 6	1985

NB In north-west Africa, the original (Arabic!) numbers have been retained: 1, 2, 3 ...

ITINERARY	
DATE	PLACE

ADDRESSES

NAME _____

ADDRESS _____

_____ PHONE _____

NAME _____

ADDRESS _____

_____ PHONE _____

NAME _____

ADDRESS _____

_____ PHONE _____

NAME _____

ADDRESS _____

_____ PHONE _____

NAME _____

ADDRESS _____

_____ PHONE _____